93690739R00075

Made in the USA
Middletown, DE
15 October 2018

The Top 2,000+ Words and Expressions for Understanding Emirati Dialect

Nasser M. Isleem ناصر إسليم

The Top 2,000+ Words and Expressions for

Understanding Emirati Dialect

In this book, you will find more than 2000 Emirati common words and expressions. It introduces the learner to the Emirati dialect spoken today in addition to aspects from the culture in the United Arab Emirates. Whether you have prior knowledge of Modern Standard Arabic or simply the desire to learn essential aspects of the spoken dialect of the UAE, this book is the one for you. It is designed to serve learners coming from different age, educational and professional backgrounds. Its content was firstly taught to non-Arab students at New York University Abu Dhabi, and is now available for Arabic language learners everywhere.

يحتوي هذا الكتيب التعليمي على أكثر من ٢٠٠٠ كلمة وتعبير إماراتي. حيث أنه يُعرّض المتعلم للمحات من اللهجة الإماراتية الدارجة اليوم. بالإضافة إلى جوانب مختلفة من الثقافة في دولة الإمارات العربية المتحدة. سواء كانت لديك المعرفة المسبقة باللغة العربية الفصحى. أو الرغبة بتعلم جوانب عدة من اللهجة الحكية في الإمارات. فهذا الكتيب هو الأمثل لك. فقد تم تصميم هذا المُنتَج كي يخدم المهتمين بشتى أطيافهم العمرية والتعليمية والمهنية. استُخدمت مادة هذا الكتيب للمرة الأولى في تعليم طلاب جامعة نيويورك أبوظبي الناطقين بغير اللغة العربية. وهو الآن متوفر لدارسي اللغة العربية في كل مكان.

Content المحتوى

Content	Page

Content	Page

The growing demand from expatriates in the UAE to learn the local dialect, the increasing number of foreign educational and business institutions and the need for a resource to be used for these unique purposes has encouraged Nasser M. Isleem to develop a new phrasebook entitled *The Top 2000+ Words and Expressions for Understanding Emirati dialect*. The new book targets learners with or without existing knowledge of Modern Standard Arabic (MSA), and teaches them target dialect through Arabic as well as transliterated text. This book introduces learners to the uniqueness of the present-day Emirati dialect and life through exposing them to essential common vocabulary, expressions and grammar notes, which are key in studying any dialect. Being a unique publication in the field of Emirati dialect learning, this book is a significant resource for individuals coming from different agegroups, educational backgrounds, as well as corporations not only in the UAE but also in the Gulf countries with populations interested in learning the local dialects in these countries. This is a unique project also because it opens a new gate into learning about the culture of this society through its presently spoken dialect, which will hopefully result in growing the conversation between the members of a very diverse community in the UAE and the Gulf in general.

Acknowledgement شكر وعرفان

Without the help and support of the following people, this book would have never become a reality. I would like to thank my wife Laila and my children. I would like to thank all of my friends and colleagues for their support, excitement, and encouragement. I am also indebted to my students at NYUAD, UNC-Chapel Hill, and Duke, who were always enthusiastic participants in my classes. I am indebted to the January Term NYUAD students who worked very hard learning from the draft of the book during the Emirati dialect and culture course over the past five years. Their positive reactions and enthusiasm for learning Emirati expressions and culture have significantly influenced me to write the book. I would like to thank those who help make the Al Ain J Term journey of learning Emirati dialect run in a smooth and easy fashion (Mr. Mohamed Al Nayadi, Huda Al Blushi and all employees of AlQattara Arts Center in Al Ain city, Ibrahim El Lababidi, Mohammed Al Dhere, Mumtaz Mahmoud, Sameera Isleem, Yasser Al Mansouri, Mohamed Mahmoud). I would also like to thank Dr. Muhamed Al Khalil and Carol Brandt for inspiring me to embrace the first project of writing my other book "Ramsah an Introduction to Learning Emirati Dialect and Culture". My gratitude is to Nidaa Samsam for her creative designing skills, and Dr. Naji Qbeilat who facilitated the design work. Last and not least, I beg forgiveness of all those who have been with me over the course of the years and whose names I have failed to mention.

Nasser M. Isleem

Nasser M. Isleem is a native of Palestine and brings many years of experience teaching all levels of Arabic language and culture at NYUAD, UNC-Chapel Hill, Duke University, Meredith College, and Durham Technical Community College. He currently teaches at NYUAD. He became a certified ACTFL OPI tester in 2010. Isleem has participated in many academic conferences where he addressed the importance of Arabic culture integration, common expressions, proverbs, and songs in Arabic language classes. Isleem is a pioneer in applying studies that examine the impact of using songs, proverbs, and other cultural expressions and components in teaching the Arabic language.

Professor Isleem has authored many other scholarly books and specializes in teaching Arabic to non-Arabic speaking students. His teaching interests include Arabic language and culture, and Egyptian, Levantine, and Gulf dialects. He is also deeply committed to offering training to language teaching practitioners in order to help them better realize their potential through the integration of culture in language teaching. He is the recipient of the Tanner University Teaching Award (UNC-Chapel Hill) in 2012 and the Order of the Golden Fleece (UNC-Chapel Hill) in 2011 and Student Undergraduate Teaching and Staff Awards (UNC-Chapel Hill) in 2006. More about Isleem's publications can be found at www.arabiyyaat.com

Arabic Alphabet and Transliteration Chart

Let's start this journey by taking a look at the transliteration chart of the Arabic alphabet that will be used in this book. Tip: Many words in this chart are related to Emirati culture! Learn how to pronounce these words:

الحرف Arabic Letter	الفصحى MSA (Modern Standard Arabic)	الإماراتية Emirati Dialect
ا	'a —› *a*nchor	'a
ب	b —› *b*ad	b
ت	t —› *t*ea	t
ث	th à *th*ink	th
ج	j —› *j*ar	j —› jar y —› yes
ح	7 —› *h*amdan	7
خ	kh —› German *ch*	kh
د	d —› *d*irham	d
ذ	dh —› *th*at	dh
ر	r —› *r*ice	r
ز	z —› *z*akat	z
س	s —› *s*un	s
ش	sh —› *sh*eep	sh
ص	S —› *S*ubtle	S
ض	D —› mu*d*	TH
ط	T —› bu*tt*on	T
ظ	TH —› *th*us	TH
ع	3 —› Ali	3
غ	gh —› French *r*	gh
ف	f —› *f*ire	f

		q → Quran
ق	q → Quran	g → goose
		j → jar
ك	k → kitchen ch chair	k / ch
ل	l → lemon	l
م	m → map	m
ن	n → needle	n
ھ	h → herd	h
و	w → wall	w
ي	y → yes	y
أ	'a – apple	'a
ء	' – 'h-'h ='uh-'uh	'
إ	'i –'inshaAllah	'i
أ	'u – orange	'u

In addition to the letters above, there are few short and long vowels that you will encounter.

Arabic Vowel	Transliteration	Example
ا	a	ban
و	uu	noon
ي	ii	feed
ـَ	a	fed
ـُ	o	long
ـِ	i	tin

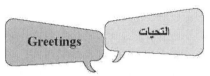

Greetings — التحيات

... الرد 'ir-rad Response		... التحية 'it-ta7iyya Greeting	
Morning الصّبح			
Seba7 'in-nuur	صباح النّور	Seba7 'il-kheir	صباح الخَيْر
Evening المِسا			
mesa 'in-nuur	مِسا النّور	mesa 'il-kheir	مِسا الخَيْر
Anytime في كُلّ وَقْت			
ya hala	يا هلا	mar7eba	مَرْحبا
mar7eb bajii	مرحَبْ باقي!	mar7eba 'is-sa3	مرحِبا الساع!
mar7eba melayiin!	مرحبا ملايين!		
wa 3aleikum 'is-salam	وَعَلَيْكم السّلام	'is-salam 3aleikum	السلامَ عَلَيْكم

أكثر عن التحيات والسؤال عن الصحة

More About Greetings and Asking About Health

Meaning المعنى	Transliteraton	Word الكلمة
Hello, what's your name? "addressed to a masculine singular = "masc. sing."	mer7eba, shismek?	مرحبا، شسمك؟
Hello, what's your name? "addressed to feminine singular = "fem. sing."	mer7eba, shismich?	مرحبا، شسمِك؟

How are you? "masc. sing."	keif 7alek?	كيف حالك؟
	sh7alek?	شحالك؟
How are you? "fem. sing."	keif 7al-ech?	كيف حالك؟
	sh7alech?	شحالك؟
Fine, Okay	zein	زين
Praise due to the Lord	'il-7amd lillah	الحمد لله
Good morning	Sab-ba7k Allah bil-kheir	صبّحك الله بالخير
Good evening	mas-sak Allah bil-kheir	مسّاك الله بالخير
Welcome (May you be greeted by God)	7ay-yakum Allah	حيّاكم الله
What is your news? (How are you doing?) "masc. sing."	shekhbarek?	شخبارك؟
	she3luumek?	شعلومك؟
What is your news? How are you doing? "fem. sing."	shekhbarech?	شخبارك؟
	she3luumech?	شعلومك؟
Welcome, Hello	mar7eba w sahla	مرحبا وسهلا
Reply to 'ahlan wa sahlan (man / woman)	hala bek / bech	هلا بك
How are you all doing?	keif 7alkum?	كيف حالكم
	sh-7alkum?	شحالكم
Hello dear	hala w ghala	هلا وغلا
Hello! lit. (Hello Hello)	hala wal-lah	هلا والله

Meaning المعنى	Transliteraton	Word الكلمة
Come in please! Here you go "masc. sing." / Come in please! "fem. sing."	'igreb / 'igrebii	اقرب / اقربي
Reply to ('igreb), it means "close, near". It is said even if the person being asked to come in does not accept to get in.	geriib / jiriib	قريب
Come in please! Here you go "masc. sing." / Come in please! "fem. sing."	tfaTHal / tfaTHalii	تفضل / تفضلي
Relpy to (tfaDHal or tfaDHalii),Thank you "masc. sing.", "fem. sing."	dam faTHlek / dam faTHlich	دام فضلك / دام فضلك
The house is yours (feel home)	'ilbeit beitek	البيت بيتك
The man who is welcoming the guest would say (houd) with a voice loud enough for women to hear and get the message.	houd	هود
Reply to (houd), said by those who are in the house as a hint that it is clear and to give permission to the guest to come in.	hida	هدا

Saying "Goodbye and Asking for Permission to Leave"

Meaning المعنى	Transliteraton	Word الكلمة
Good bye	*ma3as-salamah*	مع السلامة
	darb-'is-salamah	درب السلامة
	faman Allah	فمان الله
Reply to *(faman Allah)*	*faman 'il-kariim*	فمان الكريم

Family and Social Circle — العايلة والمحيط الاجتماعي

Meaning المعنى	Transliteraton	Word الكلمة
Father	walid	والد
Mother	waldah	والْدة
Son	wild	ولد
Daughter	bint	بنت
Brother	'akh	أخ
Sister	'ikht	إخت
Uncle	3amm	عَم
Aunt	3am-mah	عَمة
Uncle (mother's side)	khal	خال
Aunt (mom's side)	khala	خالة
Grandfather	yadd	جد
Grandmother	yad-dah	جدّة
Clan	3eshiirah	عشيرة
Tribe	jibiilah	قبيلة
Grandson	7efiid	حفيد
Granddaughter	7efiidah	حفيدة
Kid	yahil	جاهل
Brother-in-law	nisiib	نسيب
Friend	'irbii3 = Sadiig	ربيع = صديق
Neighbor	yar	جار
Children	3yal	عيال
Man	ray-yal	رجال
Woman	7ermeh	حرمة
Old man	sheibah	شيبة
Old woman	3iyuuz	عجوز

14

Married	'im-3ar-ris = mit-zaw-wij	معرس = متزوّج
Divorced	'im-Tal-lig	مطلق
Widow	'armal	أرمل
Single	3zuubii	عزوبي
My wife	7erimtii = zoujtii	حرمتي = زوجتي
My husband	raylii = zoujii	ريلي = زوجي

السؤال عن العايلة

Asking about family

Meaning المعنى	Transliteraton	Word الكلمة
How's the father (how's your father?)	sh-7al-l-walid?	شحال الوالد؟
How is your brother? "addressing masc. sing."	shekhbar 'ukhuuk?	شخبار أخوك؟
How is your grandfather? "addressing fem. sing."	sh-7al yeddich?	شحال جدك؟
How is your friend...? "masc. sing"	shu3luum rebii3ek?	شعلوم ربيعك...؟

Pronouns — الضمائر

انجليزي English	إماراتي Emirati		
I	'ana	أنا	أ + ن + ا
We	na7an	نحن	نْ + حَ + ن
You "mas. sing"	'inta	إنتَ	إ + ن + تَ
You "fem. sing."	'inti	إنتِ	إ + ن + تِ
You "plural masc."	'intu	إنتو	إ + ن + تَ + و
You "pl. fem." = (plural femenine)	'intin	إنتِن	إ + ن + تِ + ن
He	huu	هو	هـ + وْ
She	hii	هي	هـ + يّ
They (used for dual and plural masculine)	homm	هُمّ	هـ + مّ
They (used for duality and plural feminine)	hinn	هِنْ	هـِ + نْ

انجليزي / English	إماراتي / Emirati		
Condition	7al	حال	ح + ا + ل
My condition	7alii	حالي	ح + ا + ل + ي
Your cond. (masc. sing.)	7alik	حالك	ح + ا + ل + ك
Your cond. (fem. sing.)	7alich	حالك	ح + ا + ل + ك
Her condition	7alha	حالها	ح + ا + ل + هـ + ا
His condition	7alah	حاله	ح + ا + ل + ه
Their (masc.) condition	7alhom	حالهم	ح + ا + ل + هـ + م
Their (fem.) condition	7alhin	حالهن	ح + ا + ل + هـ + ن

Note: the word شكل *shakl* is a noun, which means (form, shape). In Emirati dialect, when we attach it with a suffix pronoun, it means (seem, look like)

I seem to	shaklii	شكلي
We seem to	shakelna	شكلنا
You "masc. sing." seem to	shaklek	شكلك
You "fem. sing." seem to	shaklech	شكلك
You "masc. pl." seem to	shakelkum	شكلكم
He seems	shaklah	شكله
She seems to	shakelha	شكلها
They seem to	shakelhum	شكلهم

Attached pronouns may be suffixed to مال ، مالت (belonging)

My car, the car of mine, the car belonging to me	'issayyara malti	السيارة مالتي
The house, the houses of mine	'ilbeit mali	البيت مالي
My cars, the cars of mine	'issyayiir malti	السيايير مالتي

17

Names of Emirates and Cities in the UAE

أسماء إمارات ومدن في دولة الإمارات

الإنجليزية English	Transliteration	الإمارة Emirate
UAE – The Emirates	'il-imarat	الإمارات
Abu Dhabi	buu THabii	أبوظبي
Dubai	dbai	دبي
Sharjah	'ish-sharjah	الشارقة
Ajman	3iiman	عجمان
Um Al Quwain	'um-mil-geiwein	أم القيوين
Al Fujairah	'il-fjeirah	الفجيرة
Ras Al Khaimah	ras 'il-kheimah	راس الخيمة

الإنجليزية English	Transliteration	المدينة أو الجزيرة City, Town, or Island
Al Ain	'il-3ein	العين
Kalba	kalba = chalba	كلباء
Al Marfa	'il-marfa	المرفا
Liwa	liiwa	ليوا
Khour Fakkan	khour fak-kan	خور فكان
Tunb Asoghra	Tonb 'is-Soghra	طنب الصغرى
Tunb Al Kobra	Tonb 'il-kobra	طنب الكبرى
Abu Musa	'ubuu muusa	أبو موسى
Sadiyat	'is-sa3diy-yat	السعديات
Yas	yas	ياس
Hatta	7at-ta	حتا
Ghiyathi	ghiyathii	غياثي

| Where are you from? | min wein 'inta (male)? / 'inti? (female)? | من وين أنتَ / أنتِ؟ |
| I am from Abu Dhabi, and you? | 'ana min buu THabii, winta? | أنا من بوظبي؟ وأنتَ؟ |

كلمات لها علاقة بالجنسيات الموجودة في الإمارات

Words Related to Nationalities Available in the UAE

Emirati	'imaratii	إماراتي
Local	muwaTin	مواطن
Gulf citizen	khaliijii	خليجي
Resident	muqiim	مقيم
Residency	'iqamah	إقامة
Indian	hindii	هندي
Pakistani	bakistanii	باكستاني
Iranian	'iranii	إيراني
Bengali	benghalii	بنغالي
Chinese	Siinii	صيني
Korean	kuurii	كوري
French	faransii	فرنسي
German	'almanii	ألماني
American	'amriikii	أمريكي
British	beriiTanii	بريطاني
Australian	'usturalii	أسترالي
Russian	ruusii	روسي
Italian	'iTalii	إيطالي

19

How do you feel? — keif 'il7al? — كيف الحال؟

المعنى بالإنجليزية Eng. Meaning	الجمع Plural (Pl.)		المفرد المؤنّث Fem. Sing.		المفرد المذكر Masc. Sing.	
Hot	7ar-raniin	حرّانين	7ar-ranah	حرّانة	7ar-ran	حرّان
Cold	bardaniin	بردانين	bardanah	بردانة	bardan	بَردان
Hungry	you3aniin	جُوعانين	you3anah	جُوعانة	you3an	جُوعان
	ywa3a	جُواعى				
Full, satiated	shab3aniin	شبعانين	shab3anah	شبعانة	shab3an	شْبْعان
Lazy	kaslaniin	كسلانين	kaslanah	كسلانة	kaslan	كسْلان
Bored, fed up	mal-laniin	ملآنين	mal-lanah	ملآنة	mal-lan	ملآن
	Tafraniin	طفرانين	Tafranah	طفرانة	Tafran	طفران
Sad, upset	za3laniin	زعلانين	za3lanah	زعلانة	za3lan	زَعْلان
Tired	ta3baniin	تعبانين	ta3banah	تعبانة	ta3ban	تَعْبان
Sick	meriiTHiin	مريضين	meriiTHah	مريضة	meriiTH	مريض
	meraTHa	مراضى				
Sleepy	na3saniin	نعسانين	na3sanah	نعسانة	na3san	نَعْسان

تعلموا : Learn

Feeling very scared	may-yit mn-'il khouf	ميت من الخوف
Feeling very cold	may-yit mn-'il bard	ميت من البرد
Feeling very sleepy	may-yit mn-'in-n3as	ميت من النعاس

20

In the Hospital في المستشفى

Meaning المعنى	Transliteraton	Word الكلمة
Infection	'iltihab	إلتهاب
Stomachache	maghaS	مغص
Pain	'alam / wiya3	ألم / وجع
Headache	Seda3	صداع
Diarreah	'is-hal	اسهال
Medication	duwa	دوا
Pill	7ab-bah	حبّة
Allergy	7asasiy-yah	حساسية
Fever	7im-ma	حمّى
Cold	zikam = zicham	زكام
Vomiting	zu-wa3	زواع
Cancer	saraTan	سرطان
Dizziness	doukhah	دوخة
Constipation	'imsak	إمساك
Temprature	7ararah	حرارة
injection	'ibrah	إبرة
Blood test	fa7S damm	فحص دم
full check up	fa7S shamil	فحص شامل
test result	natiijat l-fa7S	نتيجة الفحص
Laboratory	mokhtabar	مختبر
Pharmacy	Saidaliy-yah	صيدلية
X ray	'ashi-3ah	أشعة
Diabetes	sok-karii	سكري
Pressure	THaghT	ضغط
Fracture	kasir	كسر
Surgery	jira7ah	جراحة

Pregrnant	7amil	حامل
My head hurts	rasii y3aw-wirnii	راسي يعورني
Contagious	mo3dii	مُعدي

زيارة المريض

Visiting the Sick

What Do People Say When Visiting a Sick Person?

Reply الرد		Form الصيغة	
Allah ysal-limk	الله يسلّمك	salamat	سلامات
Allah ysal-limch	الله يسلمك	salamtek "masc. sing."	سلامتك
yzak Allah kheir "masc. sing."	جزاك الله خير	salamtich "fem. sing."	سلامتك
yzach Allah kheir "fem. sing."			
Allah y3afiik "masc. sing."	الله يعافيك	Tahuur 'in sha Allah	طهور إن شا الله
Allah y3afiich "fem. sing."			
'ish-sharr ma 'iyyiik	الشر ما يجيك	'ajr w 3afyah	أجر وعافية
'ish-sharr ma 'iyyiich	الشر ما يجيك	ma tshuuf sharr	ما تشوف شر
		ma tshuufiin sharr	ما تشوفين شر

22

Body Parts and Organs — أعضاء وأجزاء الجسم

Meaning المعنى	Transliteraton	الكلمة Body Part / Organ
Hand	'iid	إيد
Hands	'iidein	إيدين
Eye	3ein	عين
Nose	khashm	خشم
Noses	khshuum	خشوم
Eyebrows	7uwajib	حواجب
	7iyat	حيات
Belly	baTin	بطن
Bellies	bTuun	بطون
Tongue	lsan	لسان
Tongues	'alsina	ألسنة
Heart	galb	قلب
Hearts	gluub	قلوب
Lip	shif-fah	شفة
Lips	shefayif	شفايف
Lip	berTom	برطم
Lips	baraTim	براطم
Mustache	shanab	شنب
Mustaches	shnuub	شنوب

23

English	Transliteration	Arabic
Face	*wayh*	وجه
Faces	*wyuuh*	وجوه
Throat (mouth)	*7alj*	حلق
Throats (mouths)	*7luuj*	حلوق
Neck	*rigbah*	رقّبة
Necks	*rgab*	رقاب
Hair	*sha3ar*	شعر
Bones	*3aTHm*	عظم
Brain	*mukh*	مخ
Skin	*yild*	جلد
Foot	*riil*	رجل
Legs	*ryuul*	رجول
Head	*ras*	راس
Heads	*ruus*	روس
Mouth	*famm / thamm*	فم / ثم
Mounths	*'athami*	أثامي
Eyelash	*remsh*	رمش
Eyelashes	*rmuush*	رموش
	hedab	هدب
Tummy, Stomak	*mi3dah*	معدة
Tooth	*sinn*	سنّ
Teeth	*'asnan = snuun*	أسنان = سنون
Back Teeth	*THruus*	ضروس
Chest	*Sadr*	صدر
Chests	*Sduur*	صدور

Cheek	khadd	خدّ
Cheeks	khduud	خدود
Beard	li7yah	لحية
Beards	li7a	لحى
Ear	'idhn	إذن
Ears	'adhan	آذان
Forehead	yeb-ha	جبهة
Foreheads	ybah	جباه
Back	THahar	ظهر
Backs	THhuur	ظهور
Blood	damm	دم
Knee	rik-beh	ركبة
Shoulder	katf = chatf	كتف
Arm	'idhra3	ذراع

صفات جسدية

Body Characteristic

المعنى Meaning	Transliteraton	الكلمة Word
Moderate stature	marbuu3	مربوع
Skin color: Wheatish	7inTawii	حنطاوي
Very thin	TH3iif	ضعيف
	3aSguul	عصقول

	melyan	مليان
y	mrabrab	مربرب
	mdalgam	مدلقم
Fat	metiin	متين
	b3afyah	بعافية

Expressions Related to Body Organs

المعنى Meaning	Transliteraton	الكلمة Word
Has a good sense of humor	dam-mah khefiif	دمه خفيف
Lame!	dam-mah thejiil	دمه ثقيل
Badmouthed	lesanah Tuwiil	لسانه طويل
Flirty	3yuunah Tuwiilah / zayghah	عيونه طويلة / زايغة
Arrogant	rafi3 khashmah	رافع خشمه
Very edgy	nafsah b-khashmah	نفسه بخشمه
Beautiful / Handsome	mazyuun	مزيون
	gharshuub	غرشوب
Someone with wide black eyes	'ad3aj	أدعج
Frowning (stretching lips out)	mbarTim	مبرطم
Slip of a tongue	zal-lat lsan	زلة لسان
Over my dead body	3ala jith-thetii	على جثّتي

26

Asking About Health and Condition... More and More...

Meaning المعنى	Transliteraton	Word الكلمة
You look tired?! "addressing masc. sing." Yes, I have stomach ache	shaklak ta3ban? heih, 3indii maghaS	شكلك تعبان؟ هيه، عندي مغص
You look sick? "addressing fem. sing." Yes, I have a headache	shaklich meriiTHah? 'aiwah 3indii Soda3	شكلك مريضة؟ أيوة، عندي صداع
He looks upset? No, he is not upset, He is hungry	shaklah za3lan ? la, huu mob za3lan, huu yo3an	شكله زعلان؟ لا، هو مب زعلان، هو جوعان
I want to know	'aba 'a3ref	أبا أعرف
Does he have pain?	huu 3indah 'alam?	هو عنده ألم؟
A little	shwayy	شوي

27

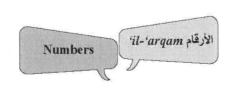

Numbers   الأرقام *'il-'arqam*

Meaning المعنى	Feminine المؤنث		Masculine المذكر	
One	*wi7dah*	وحدة	*wa7id*	واحد
Two	*thentein*	ثنتين	*'ithnein*	إثنين
Three	*thalathah (t)*	ثلاثة	*thalath*	ثلاث
Four	*'arba3ah (t)*	أربعة	*'arba3*	أرْبَع
Five	*khamsah (t)*	خمسة	*khams*	خَمْس
Six	*sit-tah (t)*	ستة	*sitt*	سِتّ
Seven	*sab3ah (t)*	سبعة	*sabe3*	سَبع
Eight	*themanyah (t)*	ثمانية	*theman*	ثَمان
Nine	*tis3ah (t)*	تسعة	*tis3*	تِسع
Ten	*3ashrah (t)*	عشرة	*3asher*	عَشر
Eleven	*7da3sh*	حْدَعْش	*7da3sh*	حْدَعْش
	7da3shar	حدعشْر	*7da3shar*	حدعشْر
Twelve	*'ithna3sh*	اثنعش	*thna3sh*	اثْنعش
	'ithna3shar	اثنعشر	*thna3shar*	اثْنعشر
Thirteen	*thalaTa3sh*	ثلطعش	*thalathTa3sh*	ثلطعش
	thalaTa3shar	ثلطعشر	*thalathTa3shar*	ثلطعشر
Fourteen	*'arba3Ta3sh*	أربعطعش	*'arba3Ta3sh*	أربعطعش
	'arba3Ta3shar	أربعطعشر	*'arba3Ta3shar*	أربعطعشر
Fifteen	*khamesta3sh*	خمستعش	*khamsTa3sh*	خمسطعش
	khamesta3shar	خمستعشر	*khamsta3shar*	خمستعشر
Sixteen	*siT-Ta3sh*	سطّعش	*sit-Ta3sh*	سطّعش
	siT-Ta3shar	سطّعشر	*sit-T-Ta3shar*	سطّعشر

Seventeen	sabe3Ta3sh	سبعطعش	sabe3Ta3sh	سبعطعش
	sabe3Ta3shar	سبعطعشر	sabe3Ta3shar	سبعطعشر
Eighteen	thimanTa3sh	ثمنطعش	thimanTa3sh	ثمنطعش
	thimanTa3shar	ثمنطعشر	thimanTa3shar	ثمنطعشر
Nineteen	tise3Ta3sh	تسعطعش	tisa3Ta3sh	تسعطعش
	tise3Ta3shar	تسعطعشر	tisa3Ta3shar	تسعطعشر
Twenty	3ishriin	عشرين	3ishriin	عشرين

Meaning المعنى	Transliteraton	Word الكلمة
Thirty	thalathiin	ثلاثين
Forty	'arbe3iin	أربعين
Fifty	khamsiin	خمسين
Sixty	sit-tiin	ستين
Seventy	sab3iin	سبعين
Eighty	themaniin	ثمانين
Ninty	tis3iin	تسعين
145	'imya w khamsa w 'arbe3iin	إمية وخمسة وأربعين
102	'imya w 'ithnein	إمية واثنين
1000	'alf	ألف
2000	'alfein	ألفين
Thousands	'aalaf	آلاف
5000	khams 'aalaf	خمس آلاف
In 2014	fii senat 'alfein w 'arba3Tash	في سنة 2014
One million	melyoun	مليون
Millions	mlayiin	ملايين

Ordinal Numbers الأعداد الترتيبية

Meaning المعنى	Transliteraton	الكلمة Word
First	*'aw-wal*	أول
Second	*thanii*	ثاني
Third	*thalith*	ثالث
Fourth	*rabi3*	رابع
Fifith	*khamis*	خامس
Sixth	*sadis*	سادس
Seventh	*sabi3*	سابع
Eighth	*thamin*	ثامن
Ninth	*tasi3*	تاسع
Tenth	*3ashir*	عاشر
The first boy	*'aw-wal walad*	أول ولد
The tenth girl	*3ashir bint*	عاشر بنت
The first one	*'aw-wal wa7id*	أول واحد
The three of them	*thalathat-hum*	ثلاثتهم
The seven of them	*sab3at-hum*	سبعتهم
The sixth (one) of them	*sadis-hum*	سادسهم
The tenth (one) of them	*3ashir-hum*	عاشرهم

Gold — الذهب

Meaning المعنى	Transliteraton	Word الكلمة
18 karat gold	*dhahab thimanTa3sh*	ذهب ثمنطعش
22 karat gold	*dhahab 'ithnein w 3ishriin*	ذهب اثنين وعشرين
24 karat gold	*dhahab 'arba3 w 3ishriin*	ذهب أربع وعشرين
Craftsmanship	*maSna3iy-yah*	مصنعية
Another form of the plural - Exaggeration	*'idh-dhihban*	الذهبان

How Much? / How Many?　　kam / cham كم

Meaning المعنى	Transliteraton	Word الكلمة
How old are you? "masc. sing.", how old are you? "fem. sing."	cham 3emrek / cham 3emrich?	كم عمرك؟ / كم عمرك
How much dirhams you have?	cham dirham ma3ak?	كم درهم معك؟
How much did you pay?	cham difa3t?	كم دفعت؟
How much is it (the bill)?	cham 'il-7isab?	كم الحساب؟
How much is it worth?	cham tiswa?	كم تسوى؟
How many men are you?	cham ray-yal 'into?	كم ريّال انتو؟
What time is it?	cham 'is-sa3ah?	كم الساعة

What time is it?

Meaning المعنى	Transliteraton	Word الكلمة
What time is it?	kam 'is-sa3ah	كم الساعة؟
Before	gabl	قبل
Quarter	rube3	ربع
Third	thilth	ثلث
Half	neS	نص
To, Till, except	'il-la	إلا
And	w	و
minute/ minutes	degiiga /degayeg	دقيقة / دقايق
Second / seconds	thanyah / thuwanii	ثانية / ثواني
Exactly	biTH-THabT	بالضبط
At night	bil-leil	بالليل
Morning	'iS-Seb7	الصبح
Noon	'iTH-THehr	الظهر
Evening	'il-mesa	المسا
Forenoon	'iTH-THe7a	الضحى
Sunset time	'il-magharb	المغرب
Before sunset	'il-3aSer	العصر
How many?	kam?	كم..؟
Now	'al7iin	الحين
Last year	'is-sineh 'il-lii Tafat	السنة اللي طافت
Last week	lisbuu3 'il-lii Taf	الأسبوع اللي طاف
Last month	'ish-shahr 'il-ii Taf	الشهر اللي طاف

33

Meaning المعنى	Transliteraton	Word الكلمة
How much is the kilo of meat?	b-kam kiilo 'il-la7am?	بكم كيلو اللحم ؟
How much is the kilo of fish?	b-cham kiilo 'is-simach?	بكم كيلو السمك ؟
How much is the kilo of tomatoes?	b-cham kiilo 'iT-TemaT?	بكم كيلو الطماطة؟
How much is the kilo of carrot?	b-cham kilo 'il-yizar?	بكم كيلو الجزر ؟

Meaning المعنى	Transliteraton	الكلمة Question word
What	sh / shuu	شـ / شنو
Where	wein	وين
Where from	min wein	من وين
Who	menuu	منو = من هو
When	meta	متى
Since when?	min meta	من متى
To whom	7ag menuu	حق منو
	mal menuu	مال منو
Which	'ayy	أي
How many, How much	kam / cham	كم
Why	leish	ليش
How	keif	كيف
	shgayil	شقايل

Meaning المعنى	Transliteraton	Expression التعبير
Where are you? "masc. sing."	*weinik?*	وينك ؟
Where are you? "fem. sing."	*weinich?*	وينك ؟
Where are you? "masc. pl."	*weinkom?*	وينكم ؟
Why are you mad? "masc. sing." Remember when you address fem. sing., you add (*ah*) to the end of adj. *(leish za3lanah?)*	*leish za3lan?*	ليش زعلان؟
Why is it prohibited?	*leish mamnuu3?*	ليش ممنوع؟
Why are you late? "masc. sing."	*leish mit'akhirr?*	ليش متأخر ؟
Explain to me, why? "masc. sing." , "fem. sing."	*fah-himnii leish?* *fahmiinii leish?*	فهمني ليش؟ فهميني ليش؟
Where is your house? "masc. sing."	*wein beitek?*	وين بيتك؟
Where is the restaurant?	*wein 'ilmaT3am?*	وين المطعم؟
Where shall we meet?	*wein binit-laga?*	وين بنتلاقى؟
Where are you going? "masc. sing."	*wein ray-ye7?*	وين رايح؟
How can I go to the market?	*keif 'asiir 'is-suug?*	كيف أسير السوق؟
How do you say such a thing? "masc. sing."	*keif 'itguul chii?*	كيف تقول كيه؟
How can I speak Emirati?	*keif 'armis 'imarati?*	كيف أرمس إماراتي؟
How come?!	*keif chii?*	كيف كيه؟
How long have you been in the UAE? 'masc. sing."	*kam = (cham) Sar lek bil'imarat?*	كم صار لك بالامارات؟

English	Transliteration	Arabic
How many do you need? "masc. sing.", "fem. sing."	kam wa7id teba? kam wa7id tebiin?	؟، كم واحد تبين؟
How many children do you have? "masc. sing.""	kam walad 3indek?	ك؟
Who is talking?	'im-nuu yitkal-lam?	منو يتكلم؟
Who sent you the news? "masc. sing."	'im-nuu Tar-rash lek-l- khabar?	منو طرش لك الخبر؟
Who is at the door?	'im-nuu 3ind-l-bab?	منو عند الباب؟
Who wants coffee?	'im-nuu yeba ga-hwah?	منو يبا قهوة؟
What are you doing? "masc. sing.", fem. sing."	shuu 'itsaw-wii? shuu 'itsaw-wiin?	شو تسوي؟ شو تسوين؟
What is the dinner? (what's is going to be served for dinner?)	shuu-l-3esha?	شو العشا؟
What's going on?	shis-salfah?	شسالفة؟
What kind of talk is this?	sh-hal-kalam?	شهالكلام؟
Which kind?	'ayy noa3?	أي نوع؟
Which one?	'ayy wa7id?	أي واحد؟
Which way (direction, side)?	'ayy Soab?	أي صوب؟
Which color?	'ayy loan?	أي لون؟

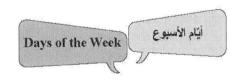

Days of the Week أيّام الأسبوع

Meaning المعنى	Transliteraton	Word الكلمة
Saturday	'is-sabt	السبت
Sunday	'il-'a7ad	الأحد
Monday	lithnein	الإثنين
Tuesday	'ith-thalatha	الثلاث
Wednesday	larbi3a	الأربعاء
Thursday	'il-khemiis	الخميس
Friday	'il-yim3a	الجمعة
After	3egob	عِقب
Today	'il-yoam	اليوم
Yesterday (morning)	'ams	أمس
The day before yesterday	'awwal 'ams	أول أمس
Yesterday (evening)	'il-bar7ah	البارحة
The day before yesterday	'aw-walt 'il-bar7ah	أولة البارحة
Tomorrow	bachir	باكر
The day after tomorrow	3egub bachir	عقب باكر
Early morning	ghebshah	غبشة
Afternoon	'il-gaylah	القايلة
Forenoon	'iTH-The7a	الضحى

Islamic Hijri Months الشهور الهجرية	
m7arram	محرم
Safar	صفر
rabii3-'il-'awwal	ربيع الأول
rabii3-'ith-th-anii	ربيع الثاني
jumada-l-'awwal	جمادى الأول
jumada-th-thanii	جمادى الثاني
rajab	رجب
sha3ban	شعبان
remTHan	رمضان
shaw-wal	شوال
dhul-qi3dah	ذو القعدة
dhul-7ij-jah	ذو الحجة

Meaning المعنى	Europenan Months الشهور الميلادية	
January	yanayir	يناير
February	fibrayir	فبراير
March	maris	مارس
April	'ibriil	إبريل
March	mayo	مايو
April	younyo	يونيو
July	yoalyo	يوليو
August	'aghosTos	أغسطس
September	sebtamber	سبتمبر
October	'uktoabar	أكتوبر
November	noafambar	نوفمبر
December	diisambar	ديسمبر

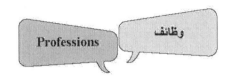

Professions وظائف

Meaning المعنى	Transliteraton	Word الكلمة
Driver	*drei-wil*	دريول
Teacher	*mudra-ris*	مُدرّس
Maid	*bosh-karah / khad-damah*	بشكارة / خدَامة
Engineer	*mohandis*	مهندس
Doctor	*Tabiib / duktuur*	طبيب / دكتور
Dentist	*Tabiib 'asnan*	طبيب أسنان
pharmacist	*Sai-dalii*	صيدلي
Nurse	*mumariTH*	ممرض
Vet	*Tabiib baiTarii*	طبيب بيطري
Technician	*fan-nii*	فني
Laborer	*3amil*	عامل
Barber	*7al-lag*	حلاق
Expert	*khabiir*	خبير
Worker	*katib*	كاتب
Secretary	*sikir-teir*	سكرتير
Policeman	*shor-Tii*	شرطي
Housewife	*rab-bat beit*	ربة بيت
Unemployed	*3aTil 3an-'il-3amal*	عاطل عن العمل
Soldier	*jin-dii*	جندي
Officer	*THabiT*	ضابط
Pilot	*Tay-yar*	طيار
Minister	*waziir*	وزير
Air host	*muTHiif Tayaran*	مضيف طيران
Admin.	*'idarii*	إداري
Baker	*khab-baz*	خباز
Mechanic	*miikaniikii*	ميكانيكي
Judge	*gaTHii*	قاضي
Manager, school principal	*mudiir*	مدير

Words and Phrases Related to Work and Professions

Meaning المعنى	Transliteraton	Word الكلمة
Boss, refined man	'arbab	أرباب
Incharge (supervisor)	mas'uul	مسؤول
Executive director	mudiir tanfiidhii	مدير تنفيذي
Division head	ra'iis qisim	رئيس قسم
Meeting	'ijtima3	اجتماع
Office	maktab	مكتب
Department, division	qisim	قسم
Conference	mo'tamar	مؤتمر
Degree	darajah	درجة
Promotion	tarqiyah	ترقية
How are things going?	keif l-'umuur?	كيف الأمور؟
Where is our meeting?	wein 'ijtima3na?	وين اجتماعنا؟
The workday is long!	'id-dewam Tuwiil!	الدوام طويل!
He went to pray	ra7 yiSalii!	راح يصلي!
He'll be back in a short while	raji3 = (radd) 3egeb shwayy	راجع = (راد) عقب شوي
I did not get any news	ma weSalnii 'ayy khabar	ما وصلني أي خبر
Not available	mob mawjuud	مب موجود
I have an appointment	3indii maw3id	عندي موعد
I need to be in...	yebalii 'akuun fii...	يبالي أكون في...
The meeting is cancelled	'itkansel 'il-ijtima3	اتكنسل الاجتماع
What's the plan?	shuu 'il-khiT-Tah?	شو الخطة؟
Little work, easy work	sheghel khafiif	شغل خفيف

41

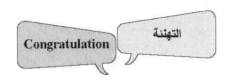

Congratulation — التهنئة

Reply الرد	Form of Congratulation التهنئة
Ramadan رمضان	
علينا وعليكم	مبروك عليكم الشهر
3aleina w 3aleikum	*mabruuk 3eleikom 'ish-shahr*
Upon us and you	Blessed is your Ramadan
Eid العيد	
علينا وعليكم	مبارك عيدكم أو عيدكم مبارك
3aleina w 3aleikum	*mbarakin 3iidkum* or
	3iidkum mbarak
Upon us and you	Blessed is your Eid
من عواده وفوّازه	عساكم من عواده / العايدين
أو من العايدين والفايزين	
min 3uw-wadah w fuw-wazah or	*3asakum min*
min 'il-3aydiin w 'il-faiziin	*3uw-wadah / 'il-3aydiin*
Expression said in reply to "Happy "Eid	Many happy returns

العمرة والحج Umrah and Haj	
منا ومنكم *minna wa minkom* From us and you	عمرة مقبولة *3umrah magbuula* حج مقبول *7aj magbuul* May God accept your Umrah (Haj)
سقوط المطر Rain Fall	
الله يبارك فيك *Allah ybarek fiik* God bless you!	مبروك عليكم الرحمة *mabruuk 3eleikum 'ir-ra7ma* Congratulation for the mercy!
مولود جديد New Born Baby	
الله يبارك فيك *Allah ybarek fiik* May God bless you	مبروك ما جاكم *mabruuk ma yakum* Congratulations for the comer (the baby)
شراء بيت جديد Buying New House	
الله يبارك فيك *Allah ybarek fiik* May God bless you "masc. sing."	عساه بيت مبارك *3esah beitin mbarek* Congratulations for the house
الفوز بمباراة، سباق هجن أو غيره (Winning (a Game, Camel Race etc	
الله يبارك فيك *Allah ybarek fiik* May God bless you "masc. sing."	مبروك الفوز *mabruuk 'il-foaz* Congratulations for winning بالبركة *bil-brukah* Congratulations!

43

Meaning المعنى	Transliteraton	Word الكلمة
Ticket	*tadhkara*	تذكرة
Round trip	*dhahab w 'iyaab*	ذهاب وإياب
	rou7a w rad-dah	روحة وردّة
Take off	*Tela3 - yeTla3*	طلع - يطلع
Arrive	*weSal -yoaSal*	وصل - يوصل

Saying Goodbye الوداع		
Meaning المعنى	Transliteraton	Word الكلمة
Goodbye	*feman Allah*	فمان الله
Goodbye	*feman l-kariim*	فمان الكريم

44

Vocabulary Related to Wedding Celebration

مفردات لها علاقة بالأعراس

Meaning المعنى	Transliteraton	Word الكلمة
Engagement	khuTuubah	خطوبة
Bride	3aruus	عروس
Groom	3ariis	عريس
Bride's family and groom's family	'ahl 'il-3aruus w 'ahl 'il mi3ris	أهل العروس وأهل المعرس
Official engagement	mil-cheh	ملكة
Wedding celebration	7aflit 3irs	حفلة عرس
Henna night	leilat 'il-7in-na	ليلة الحنا
Guests	ma3aziim	معازيم
Hall	qa3ah	قاعة
Wedding stage	koashah	كوشة

الزواج (ماذا يقول الناس للعريس؟)

Wedding (What Do People Say to Groom?)

Meaning المعنى	Transliteraton	التهنئة Form of congratulation
Congratulations!	bel-mbarak / mabruuk	بلمبارك / مبروك
Congratulation! From you comes the money, and from her come the kids.	mink 'il-mal w minha l-3yal	منك المال ومنها العيال
Congratulations! Hope your first baby is a boy!	bikrek walad ya mi3ris	بكرك ولد يا معرس

45

Meaning المعنى	Transliteraton	Word الكلمة
May God grant you happiness!	*Allah yis3idch*	الله يسعدك
Congratulations!	*bel-mbarak / mabruuk*	بلمبارك / مبروك
May your marriage is happy and blessed	*y3al-lah s3iid w mbarak*	يعلّه سعيد ومبارك
May the rest of the girls come next!	*3igbal 'il-bajyat*	عقبال الباقيات

Condolences   التعزية

Meaning المعنى	Transliteraton	Word الكلمة
May God make your reward greater (in heaven). This expression is said by someone to offer condolences to the deceased family	*3aTH-THam Allah 'ajerkom*	عظّم الله أجركم
Roughly means that Allah is eternal.	*'il-bega lillah*	البقاء لله
Your reward and ours. Reply to *3aTH-THam Allah 'ajerkom*	*'ajerna w 'ajrek*	أجرنا وأجرك

Meaning المعنى	Transliteraton	Word الكلمة
Please "masc. sing."	dekhiilik	دخيلك
You're welcome. As you wish "masc. sing."	falik Tayyib	فالك طيب
For the love of God then the love of you!"masc. sing."	'ana dakhil 3ala Allah thum 3leik	أنا داخل على الله ثم عليك
Literally "You fell down standing", You got it, You will have what you ask for. "masc. sing."	Ti7t wagif	طحت واقف
Help!	'il-faz3ah	الفزعة
You got it	'abshir	أبشر

أكثر عن طلب المساعدة والعشم

More about Asking for Help and Expectation

Meaning المعنى	Transliteraton	Word الكلمة
This is our good expectation of you	hadha l-3asham fiikum	هذا العشم فيكم
I'm expecting all goodness from you "masc. sing."	mit3ash-shim bik kheir	متعشم بك خير
Meeting the good expectation	3ala gadd l-3asham	على قد العشم
This was not my expectation of you	ma kan l-3asham	ما كان العشم
I had high expectations of …	3ash-shamt nafsii	عشمت نفسي
shame! Do not worry about it!	'afa 3aleik	أفا عليك

47

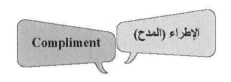

Compliment — الإطراء (المدح)

Meaning المعنى	Transliteraton	Word الكلمة
Blessings, an expression for praising when mentioning someone with good traits	win-ni3m wa Allah	والنعم والله!
He is perfect	ma 3aleih zoad	ما عليه زود
A wind blow (he's fast when it comes to offering help)	hab rii7	هب ريح
Someone with your qualities	mithlek w sherwak	مثلك وشرواك

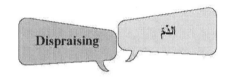

Dispraising — الذَمّ

Meaning المعنى	Transliteraton	Word الكلمة
Lit. meaning (He brought dishonor to us)	saw-wada Allah wayheh	سوّد الله وجهه
He has no honor (dignity)	ma fiih mrw-wah	ما فيه مروّة

Meaning المعنى	Transliteraton	Word الكلمة
Oh! exclamation of displeasure and it is used to express despair	*'uff*	أف
Oh! God	*'uff ya Allah!*	أف يا الله!
enough (out of you), stop it!	*bas-sik 3ad!*	بسّك عاد!
Let him go to Hell!	*khal-liih yawl-lii*	خلّيه يولّي
I need action, I became fed up with words.	*'aba fi3l shiba3t min 'il-kalam*	أبا فعل، شبعت من الكلام
Your talk makes me sick	*kalamak ymar-riTHnii*	كلامك يمرّضني

49

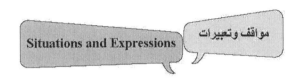

المعنى Meaning	Transliteraton	الكلمة Word
الرجاء والطلب Request		
If you please!	*law sema7t*	لو سمحت
Is it possible	*mumkin*	ممكن
with your permission	*ba3ad 'idhnik*	بعد إذنك
الاعتذار Appology		
Sorry	*'aasif*	آسف
Sorry	*7ag-gik 3alayy*	حقّك عليّ
Sorry	*'is-semuu7a*	السموحة
الرفض Rejection		
Sorry, I can't!	*'aasif ma 'aruum*	آسف ما أروم
القبول Acceptance		
Gladly! / Gladly	*min 3yuunii*	من عيوني
	'int tamer	إنت تآمر
	3ala rasii w 3eini	على راسي وعيني
المدح Praise		
Wow! Glory be to God!	*mashaAllah!*	ما شاء الله!
Glory be to God!	*tabarak ir-ra7man*	تبارك الرحمن
التعجب Admiration		
Oh God!	*mashAllah*	ما شاء الله
Oh my God!	*ya Allah!*	يا الله!

Common Phrases Used in Different Situations

	Meaning المعنى	Transliteraton	Word الكلمة
Being Full	I ate till I became full	'il7amdulil-lah, kaleit lein sheba3t	الحمد لله، كليت لين شبعت
Feeling Hungry, Food	I am hungry and I will eat a (whole) camel!	yo3an w bakil b3iir!	جوعان وباكل بعير!
	Starving	may-yit min 'il-yuu3	ميت من الجوع
	I want more	'aba ba3ed	أبا بعد
	Bon appetit!	bil-3afiyeh	بالعافية
	Fat paunches have lean pates	3ind l-buTuun ti3mal-3yuun	عِنْد البطونْ تعمى العيون
	No shaking hands while eating	la salaam 3ala Ta3am	لا سَلامْ على طعامْ
Feeling Tired	I am tired and have no strength	ta3ban w ma fiy-ya 7eil	تعبان وما فيّ حيل
	Feeling very exhausted	may-yit mn-'itt-i3ab	ميت من التعب
Feeling Bored	I am very bored! Let's go out.	Tafran wayid! yalla niTla3	طفران واجد! يلا نطلع
Offering Help	Can I help you?	tamir shayy?	تأمر شي؟
	Can I help you with something?	'agdar 'asa3dik b-shayy?	أقدر أساعدك بشي؟
	At your service	te7t 'amrak	تحت أمرك
Feeling Sorry	Unfortunately	lil'asaf	للأسف
	What a pity!	7asafah	حسافة
	Unluckily	lisuu'il-7aTH	لسوء الحظ

51

		Allah... Allah	الله... الله
Expressing Amazement/ Admiration	By God! It is stunning! (drives you nuts)	wa Allah, tkhab-bil!	والله تخبّل!
	There goes / go...!	ya salam 3ala + pronoun	يا سلام على + pro- noun
	How fortunate you are!	ya 7aTH-THik	يا حظّك
	Usually said of admiration when seeing something beautiful	tabaraka Allah	تبارك الله
Expressing Surrender and Submission to God's Will	This is God's will	hadha 'amr Allah	هاذا أمر الله
	Perished life	dinya fanya	دنيا فانية
	You will get nothing but your fated share	gheir neSiibek ma ySiibek	غير تصيبك ما يصيبك
	Glory be (referring to God) to the one who does not forget	jal-la men la yas-huu	جلّ مَن لا يَسْهو
Giving Advice, and Wishing Guidance	May God guide you "to the right path"	Allah yihdiik, Al-lah yhadak!	الله يهديك = الله يهداك!
	You have your own mind, do as you wish	3aglek b-raasek ti3ref khalaaSek	عقلك براسك تعْرف خلاصك
Request	I have a simple request!	3indi Talab besiiT	عندي طلب بسيط
	I am at your service!	min l-yedd hai lein l-yedd hai	مِن اليَدّ هاي لين اليَدّ هاي

52

Consent and Approval	That's O.K. It does not matter	*ma ykhalif*	ما يخالف
	O.K.	*ma 3aleih*	ما عليه
	Okay	*7aTHir*	حاضر
	For my part, I agree	*min Soabii, 'ana mwafig*	من صوبي، أنا موافق
	At your disposal	*ta7at taSar-rufk*	تحت تصرفك
	Consider it done, I will do it willingly	*3ala hal khashm*	على هالخشم
Scolding	He does not deserve anything	*ma yistahel shayy*	ما يستاهل شي
	Shut up! You have no manners	*Sik thamk! ma fiik 7iyah*	صك ثمك! ما فيك حيا
	Shame on you!	*7aram 3aleik*	حرام عليك
	Shame on you!	*'isti7ii 3ala wayhek! 3eib 3leik!*	استحي على وجهك! عيب عليك!
	Damn you!	*Allah ygharbilk*	الله يغربلك
	Damn you!	*Allah yil3ank*	الله يلعنّك
	Let him go to Hell!	*jhannem 'il-7amrah teTwiih*	جهنّم الْحَمّرا تطْويه
Praising	He deserves the best	*yistahel kill kheir*	يستاهل كل خير
	He has no equal	*ma leh methiil!*	ما له مثيل!
	By God! You've done more than enough	*wallah ma gaS-Sart*	والله ما قصرت
Expressing Puzzlement, Disappointment / Feeling Despair	There is no use, no one is listening (lit. whom Will I tell and whom will I talk to?")	*'aguul 7ag menuu wil-la menu*	أقول حق منو ولا منو
	Where do I go, whom should I turn to?	*wein 'aw-wal-lii, wein aruu7*	وين أولّي وين أروح
	He let me down	*fash-shalnii*	فشّلني

Problems	Do not be concerned!	la t7atii wa la yhim-mek	لا تحاتي ولا يهمّك
	Take it easy, feel comfortable!, as you wish	3ala ra7atk!	على راحتك!
	It is almost over!	hanat	هانت!
	I have a problem	3indii mishklah	عندي مشكلة
	I need a solution	'aba 7all	أبا حل
	I have a suggestion	3indii 'iqtira7	عندي اقتراح
	In my opinion	fii ra'iyii	في رأيي
	It is not my intention	mob qaSdii	مب قصدي
	Do not misunderstand me	la tifhamnii ghalaT	لا تفهمني غلط
	Do not make it worse	la tkab-bir 'il ma-wTHuu3	لا تكبّر الموضوع
	It is not worth it	'il-maw-THuu3 mob mistahill	الموضوع مب مستاهل
Craving	I wish	khaTri	خاطري في...
	How nice "to have" ..	ya salam 3ala...	يا سلام على + ...
Longing and Eagerness	I have been missing you!	mishtag lik "lich, fem. sing."	مشتاق لك
	You triggered eagerness in me	shaw-wagtnii "--tiinii, fem. sing."	شوقتني / --تيني
	I am unable to wait	mob gadir 'anti-THir	مب قادر أنتظر
	What a precious thing are the good old days!	Allah 3ala 'ayyam zaman!	الله على أيام زمان!
	I miss you	walhan 3aleik (3aleich, fem. sing."	ولهان عليك
Doubt	Is that true?	Sidg, Sidj	صدق!
	For sure?	'akiid	أكيد!
Opinion	In my opinion	fii ra'yii, fii na-THarii	في رأيي، في نظري

Prayer	My God!	*ya rabb = ya rabbi*	يا رب، يا ربي
	Promise?	*wa3d?*	وعد؟
	Completed "consider it done"	*tamm*	تمّ!
	He always breaks his promise	*dayman yikhlif!*	دايمًا يخلف!
Promise	His word is his bond	*kilimtah wi7da*	كلمته وخّدة
	The promise of the noble man is a debt on him	*wa3d 'il-7urr dein*	وعد الحُرّ دين
Compliment (to the Way Someone Looks)	You look elegant	*sh-ha-l-kashkha!*	شْهالكَشْخَة!
	How nice it is!	*sh7alatah!*	شحلاته!
	The decision is yours	*'ish-shour shourek*	الشور شورك
Choice	As you wish	*3ala keifek*	على كيفك
	Do whatever you wish	*'illii tebah*	اللي تباه
Need	It's of no concern to me	*ma lah luzuum / lazmah*	ما له لزوم / لزمه
	Required, No necessity	*lazim # mob lazim*	لازم # مب لازم
Asking Someone to Hurry up	Hurry up!	*khiff riilik!*	خف رجلك!
Slow Down	Slow down	*khaffif 'is-sir3a la tisri3!*	خفف السرعة لا تسرع!
	Fools rush in	*li3-yaleh min 'isheiTan*	العُجْلة من الشّيطان

55

Luck	God be with you, Good luck!	*Allah wyak*	الله وياك
	He has the devil's own luck	*7aTH-THah ykas-sir l-7eSa*	حظّه يكسّر الحصى
	Better luck next time	*kheirha b-gheirha*	خيرها بغيرها
	Cats have nine lives!	*shara l-gaTo*	شرا القطو
Feeling Annoyed / Angry	Beyond my ability	*foag Tagtii*	فوق طاقتي
	heavy load	*7iml thegiil*	حمل ثقيل
	He annoyed me a lot	*qeharni / geharni wayid*	قهرني واجد
	I went through hell!	*dhigt 'il-morr*	ذقت المرّ
	She destroyed me	*dam-maratni!*	دمّرتني!
	He lost his mind	*Tar 3agleh*	طار عقله
Feeling Pleased or Comfortable	Living very comfortably, doing very well	*foag 'in-nakhal*	فوق النخل
	May God be pleased with you!	*Allah yirTHa 3leik*	الله يرضى عليك
	How great and wonderful you are!	*Allah yer7am waleik*	الله يرحم والديك
Living Modestly	Living humbly, In accordance to capability	*3ala gad 'il-7al*	على قد الحال
Blame	You are in the wrong	*'il-7agg 3aleik*	الحق عليك
	These problems are caused by you	*kil-lah min te7t rasek!*	كلّه من تحت راسك!
	You are in the wrong, brother!	*ma ma3ak 7ag ya 'akhii!*	ما معك حق يا أخي!
	I blame you!	*3atban 3leik*	عتبان عليك
	He is not to be blamed!	*ma 3eleih 3itab*	ما عليه عتاب
Being in Full Control	I am in control of the situation	*'imSayTir 3al-waTHi3*	مصيطر على الوضع

56

Threatening	Don't cross the limits!	*la tit3ad-da 'il-7uduud*	لا تتعدى الحدود!
	Beat it!	*rawiina megfak*	راوينا مݠفاك
	To this limit and enough	*lein hni w-bess*	لين هْني وبسّ
Forgiveness	I made a mistake and I ask your forgiveness	*'ana mikhTi w-astasmi7 mink*	آنا مخطي واستمسح منك
	God forgives the past sin	*3efa Allah 3em-ma sellaf*	عَفا الله عَمّا سلفْ
	Let bygones be bygones	*'illi fat... mat*	اللي فاتْ ... ماتْ
	It is over now!	*shayy w-stiwa*	شي واستوى
Flexibility	Give and take (Be flexible)	*khidh w-a3Ti*	خذ وعطي
Patience	Be patient!	*Taw-wil balak!*	طوّل بالك!
	patience is the key to a happy ending	*'iSabir mifta7 'il-faraj*	الصبر مفتاح الفرج
	Rome was not built in a day	*Allah khaleg-ha b-sitt 'ay-yam*	الله خلݠها بِستّ أيّام
	Patience on a monument	*Sabr 'ayuub*	صَبر أيّوب
	Say: "peace be upon the prophet" (Be calm and Patient)	*Sall 3ala 'il-nabi*	صَلّ على النّبي
Uncertainity and Hesitation	It dpends!	*7asab = yi3timid*	حسب = يعتّمد
	Possible!	*yimkin = momkin*	يمكن = ممكن
	I do not know!	*ma-drii!*	ما ادري!

57

Mind Own Business	It's not of your business	*ma lek dakhl = ma lek khaS*	ما لك دخَل = ما لك خصّ
		ruu7, khal-lek fii 7alek "masc. sing." *ruu7ii, khal-lich fii halich,* "fem. sing."	روح، خلّك في حالك / روحي، خلك في حالك
Respect / Disrespect	Gladly, willingly	*3ala r-ras wi l-3ein*	على الراس والعين
	He fell off my eye	*Taa7 min 3eini*	طاح من عيني
	O' stranger! Be polite	*ya ghariib kuun 'adiib*	يا غريبْ كون أديبْ
Asking Someone to Be Silent	Shut up	*'iskit!*	!امسكت
	Keep your tongue inside (your mouth)	*yaw-wid lsanek*	جوّد لسانك
	Cut it off!	*Tubb 'is-salfah*	طُبّ السّالفة
Envy	Envy eats nothing but its own	*'il-7esuud la yesuud*	الحَسود لا يسُود
	They envied him	*THarbuuh b-3ein*	ضرّبوهْ بْعينْ
	May the envious, evil eye be poked with a thorn	*3ein 'il-7asuud fiiha 3uud*	عينِ الحَسود فيها عود
	Say *mashaAllah*	*guul masha Allah*	قول ما شا الله
Gossip	Don't talk so much	*la tkath-thir 'il-kalam!*	!لا تكثّر الكلام
	If speech is silver, silence is golden	*'idha kana-l-kalam min fiTH-THah fas-skuut min dhahab*	إذا كان الكلام مِن فِضّة فالسُّكوت من ذهَب..
	Reign your tongue	*lesanek 7iSanek*	لسانكْ حصانكْ
Negotiation of Agreements	If we put the conditions on the table, we will end the deal happily	*'illi 'aw-walah sharT taliih nuur*	اللي أوّله شَرْطْ تاليه نور

Politeness	If you have no shame, do whatever you please	*idha lam tasta7i faSna3 ma shi-'t*	إذا لم تستحِ فاصنعْ ما شِئْتَ
	The loud laugh bespeaks the vacant mind	*THe7k min gheir sebab gillet 'adab*	ضحْك من غير سببٌ قلة أدبْ
Keeping Low Profile	Keep the issue hidden	*'ustor 3ala ma rait*	أستُرْ على ماريت
Fear	He urinated under himself (out of fear)	*bal ta7tah*	بال تحْته
	I got so scared!	*gaff sh3r yambi*	قف شعر جمبي
	Scared to death!	*mitraw-wi3*	مِتْروّعْ
Generousity and Doing Good Deeds	a place of generosity	*beit karam*	بيت كرَم
	I appreciate your generosity	*kheirak waSil*	خيرك واصِل
	He gives twice who gives quickly	*khayrol-bir-ri 3ajeluh*	خير البرّ عاجِلُهْ
Equiality	describes the strinking similarity between two people who "come from the same mould"	*min Tiina we7da*	من طينة وَحدة
	To be in the same boat	*killna fil-hewa sewa*	كلْنا في الهوى سوا
	We are all children of Adam	*killna 3yal 'adam*	كلْنا عيال آدم
Caution	Be Alert!	*t7adh-dher*	تحَذّر
Neighbors	A good neighbor, a good morrow	*yarak 'il-geriib wa la 'ukhnak 'il-be3iid*	جارَكَ القريب ولا أخوك البعيد
Cowardice	He brought the wolf by its tail	*yaab 'idhiib min dheilah*	جاب الذّيب من ذيْله
Intelligence	genius, clever	*7adhij = feTiin*	حاذِقْ = فطين

59

Buying New Clothes	good health (said to buyer of new clothes)	*thoub l-3afiyah*	ثوب العافية
Lying	The rope of a lie is short	*7ebl 'il-chidhib geSiir*	خبل الكِذب قصير
	He who lies once, will lie every time	*min chedheb mar-rah, chedheb kill mar-rah*	مِن كِذبْ مَرّة، كذب كلّ مرة
Carelessness	Be extremely careless	*7eT fii 'idhin Tiin w-'idhin 3ayiin*	حطّ في أذن طين وأذن عجين
	He cares more or less	*la sayil w-la mistasiil*	لا سايِل ولا مِسْتسيلْ
Trust	The thief is the guard	*7amiiha 7aramiiha*	حاميها خَراميها
	Imposter	*naS=Sab = 7aiyyal*	نصّاب = حيّال
	He is dishonest	*dhim-mtah barda*	ذِمّته باردةٌ
	You can never trust him	*ma lah 'aman*	ما لهُ أمان
	Gain gotten by a lie, will burn one's finger	*maal 'il-7eram ma yiduum*	مال الحرام ما يدوم
Stupidity	Stupid	*khiblah*	خِبْلة
	Drum (Stupid)	*Tabl*	طبل
Arrogance	He is haughty	*yitkal-lem min ras khashmeh*	يتكلم من راس خشمه
	He sees (everything in) himself	*shayif 3emrah*	شايِفْ عِمْرة
Courage	Courageous	*khuu sham-ma*	خُو شَمّا
Moderation	The best (one) of issues is the moderate one	*khayr 'il-'umuur-l-wasaT*	خيْر الأمور الوَسطْ
Taking Responsibility For Actions	Evil be to you, who evil thinks	*dhanbek 3a yanbmek*	ذنْبك ع جنْبك

Gluttonousness	His stomach is his main worry	*bTeini*	بْطيني
Parents	*God›s pleasure is taken from the pleasure of parents*	*reTHa Allah min reTHa-l-waldein*	رضا الله من رضا الوالدين
	He who has children will never die	*min khel-laf ma mat*	من خلّف ما مات
Friendship	A friendship of camels (never lasting friendship)	*rib3et boush*	رِبْعة بوش
	Keep good company and you shall be one of them	*rafij-l-mesa3iid tis3ed*	رافِقْ المساعيد تِسْعَد
	Friend in need is friend indeed	*rbii3ek khashmek*	ربيعك خَشْمك
	Long life together	*3eshret 3emr*	عِشْرَةُ عمر
Secrets	Your secret's safe with me	*sid-dek fi-l 7ifTH*	سِكّكْ في الحِفْظْ
	box (good at keeping a secret)	*Senduug*	صندوق
	In a low profile!	*min te7t-l-te7t*	من تحْت لتحْت
Consolation and Encouragement to Be Strong	Pull your strength together	*shidd 7eilek*	شِدّ حيلك
Stubborness	His decision comes from his throat	*shoarah fii zoarah*	شُّورَة في زورَة
Easiness	Piece of cake	*sherabt ma'*	شّرْبَةُ ماء

Hospitality	Serve the coffee starting from your right side even if Abu Zeid (a well-known Arabian knight from Banu Hilal) sits on your left side	*Sobb l-gahwa 3ala ymiinek w-lau buu zeid 3ala ysarek*	صُبّ القَهْوة على يمينك ولو أبو زيد ع يسارَك
	No stranger except Satan	*ma gheriib 'illa 'ashiTan*	ما غريب إلا الشَّيطان
	The house is your house (feel home)	*'id-dar darak = 'il-beit beitak*	الدار دراك = البيت بيتك
Telling Truth	Truth hurts	*chelmet-l-7eg t3aw-wir*	كَلِمة الحَقّ تعوّر
Fate and Destiny	Everything is fated and destined	*kill shayy gismeh w-naSiib*	كلّ شَي قِسْمَة ونصيب
Presistence	Where there is a will, there is a way	*kill man sar 3ala-d-darb wuSal*	كلّ من سار على الدّرْب وصَل
Tardiness	Every cloud has a silver lining	*kill ta'khiira w-fiiha khiira*	كلّ تأخيرَة وفيها خيرَةٌ
Doing Favor	To be rewarded by getting nothing back	*ma yethmer fiih-l-ma3ruuf*	ما يِثْمِر فيه المَعروفْ
	Do not provide for a stingy person	*ma yukhdam bekhiil*	ما يُخدَم بخيل
Taking Revenge	Tit for tat	*we7deh b-we7deh*	وحدة بْوحدةٌ
Disgust	Disgusting thing!	*y-law-wi3 l-chabd*	يلوّع الكَبْد
Cheating	He wags his tail	*yil3eb-'ib-dheilah*	يلعب بذيلة
Challenge	It is either me or him	*ya 'ana ya huu*	يا أنا، يا هُوّ
Astonishment	Oh my God!	*ya sob7ana Allah!*	يا سُبْحان الله!
Cooperation	There is no "I" in team	*yedd wa7dah ma tSaf-fig*	يد واحدة ما تصفق

Love	Sweatheart!	*7abiibii* "masc. sing.", *7abiibtii* "fem. sing."	حبيبي / حبيبتي
	Kiss (noun)	*bousah*	بوسة
	I love	*'amuut fii, 'ad-huub fii, 'a7ib*	أموت في = أذوب في = أحب
	I would sacrifice my soul for you	*fi-deitik* " masc. sing." "--tich, "fem. sing."	فديتك
	My heart!	*ya galbii*	يا قلبي
	My life!	*3emrii, 7ayatii*	عمري / حياتي

More and More of Expressions and Replies

'il-7amdil-lah 3ala 'as-salamah الحمد لله على السلامة

Said upon returning from a trip safely and to a recovered person from sickness.

الله يسلمك

Allah ysalmik "masc. sing." / ysallimch "fem. sing."

na3iiman نعيمًا

Said to someone who just took a shower or had a haircut.

الله ينعم عليك

Allah yin3im 3aleik

جزاك الله خير yizak Allah kheir

جزانا وإيّاكم

yizana w-yakom

(may God reward you!)

بيّض الله وجهك bay-yaTH Allah wayhek

وجهك أبيض

Said to someone who brings good news or to someone who does the listener a favor.

wayhek 'abyaTH

'il-7amd lil-lah / 'il-7amdil-lah الحمد لله

يرحمك الله yir7amk Allah

Praise be to Allah

May God have mercy on you (Expression that can be said to someone who just sneezed)

قرّت عينك *gar-rat 3einek*

Lit: Your eyes are relieved

meaning you are now satisfied with your beloveds' safe comeback.

بوجه نبيّك *bwayh nebiy-yek*

Lit: Relieved by seeing the face of your prophet

لبيت حاج / حاج *lab-beit 7ajj / 7aii*

لبيت في مكة *lab-beit f-mak-kah*

May you become a pilgrim

لبيه *lab-beih*

Here I come!

عدوّك الريح *3aduw-wik 'ir-rii7*

Lit. Your enemy is the wind

استريح *'isterii7*

Have rest, Relax

وانت بكرامة *winta bkaramah*

Excuse me for the expression, word. Said to the listener upon mentioning something low in class like shoes, dog, donkey etc.

بسم الله *bismil-lah*

Said when starting anything, eating, drinking, etc.

65

The Prayers 'iSalawat الصلوات

'il-'adhan الأذان

Calling for Prayer

Meaning المعنى	Transliteraton	Word الكلمة
God is great, God is great	*Allah-o 'akbar , Allah-o 'akbar*	الله أكبر ، الله أكبر
I bear witness that there is no god but Allah	*'ash-hado 'an la 'ilaha 'il-la Allah*	أشهد أن لا إله إلا الله، أشهد أن لا إله إلا الله
I bear witness that Mohammed is the messenger of Allah	*'ash-hado 'an-na mu7am-madan ra-suulu Allah*	أشهد أن محمدًا رسول الله، أشهد أن محمدًا رسول الله
Come to prayer, come to prayer	*7ay-ya 3ala-Salah , 7ay-ya 3ala-Salah*	حيّ على الصلاة، حيّ على الصلاة
Come to success, come to success	*7ay-ya 3ala-l-falah , 7ay-ya 3ala-l-falah*	حيّ على الفلاح، حيّ على الفلاح
God is great, God is great	*Allah-o 'akbar , Allah-o 'akbar*	الله أكبر ، الله أكبر
There is no god but Allah	*la 'ilaha 'il-la Allah*	لا إله إلا الله
fayir prayer includes one line to the top *'adhan* and that is		
Prayer is better than sleep	*'aSalatu khairun mina nawm*	الصلاة خير من النوم

Swearing الطلفان

Meaning المعنى	Transliteraton	Word الكلمة
By God!	*wal-lah*	والله
By the Great God!	*wal-la-l-3aTHiim*	والله العظيم
I swear by God!	*qasam bil-lah*	قسم بالله
By the Lord of the Kabaa!	*w rabb 'il-ka3bah*	ورب الكعبة
By the name of the Lord of the House "referring the Kaaba"!	*w rabb 'il-beit*	ورب البيت
By the noble Quran!	*wil muS7af 'ish-sheriif*	والمصحف الشريف
By your head!	*w rasik*	وراسك
By the head of my mother and my father!	*w ras 'um-mi w-'ubuɯyah*	وراس أمي وأبويه
Interestingly, *wal-lah*—the most commonly used in swearing—can be used for many other purposes. Let us explore some of them here:		
Really? Seriously?	*wal-lah!* *bidh-dhim-mah?*	والله؟ بالذمة؟
You've got to be kidding me!		والله!
Oh My God! How great! Awesome!	*Allah!*	الله!!!
By The Great God... (Threatening / Serious promise)	*wa Allah-l 3aTHiim*	والله العظيم...

67

Hobbies hiwayat هوايات

Meaning المعنى	Transliteraton	Word الكلمة
Fishing	*Seid / 7adag*	صيد / حداق
Cooking	*Tabkh*	طبخ
Singing	*ghi-na*	غنا
Dancing	*ragS*	رقص
Swimming	*siba7a*	سباحة
Camel race	*sibag hijn*	سباق هجن
Car race	*sibag siy-yarat*	سباق سيارات
Drifting	*taf7iiT*	تفحيط
Reading	*girayah*	قراية
Acting	*tamthiil*	تمثيل

68

المعنى Meaning	Transliteraton	الكلمة Word
Soccer	*kurat qadam*	كرة قدم
Match	*mubarah*	مباراة
Goalkeeper	*7aris*	حارس
Player	*la3ib*	لاعب
Referee	*7akam*	حكم
Team	*fariiq*	فريق
Replacement	*'i7tiyaT*	احتياط
Trainer	*mudar-rib*	مدرب
Championship	*buTuulah*	بطولة
League	*daw-rii*	دوري
Loss	*khasarah*	خسارة
Winning	*foaz*	فوز
Cup	*kas*	كأس
Warning	*'indhar*	إنذار
Red card	*biTaqa hamra*	بطاقة حمرا
Yellow card	*biTaqa Safra*	بطاقة صفرا
Fan	*mushaj-ji3*	مشجع
Gold medal	*miidaliyah dhahabiy-yah*	ميدالية ذهبية
Silver medal	*miidaliyah fiTH-THiy-yah*	ميدالية فضبية
Net	*shabakah*	شبكة
Playground	*mal3ab*	ملعب
Club	*nadii*	نادي
Competition	*munafasah*	منافسة
Crowd	*jumhuur*	جمهور
Stadium	*'istad*	إستاد
Wenger	*jena7*	جناح
Defender - defence	*mdafi3 – difa3*	مدافع - دفاع
Midfield	*khaT wasaT*	خط وسط

Forward	hujuum - muhajim	هجوم - مهاجم
Center Forward (literally Spearhead)	ra's 7arbah	رأس حربة

Meaning المعنى	Transliteraton	Word الكلمة
How nice! (Excellent, May God protect you!)	Allah 3aleik	الله عليك
Literaly means "he shares the ball". Often said when a player skillfully handles the ball with confidence with his team-mates."	w-ywazzzzzzza3	ويوزززززززع
How nice you are (you beloved of your parents)!	Allah 3aleik ya 7abiib waldeik	الله عليك يا حبيب والديك!
How wonderful! A good kick and a better ball blocking!	ya salam! shoaTah 7ilwah w-Sad-da 'a7la	يا سلام! شوطة حلوة وصدّة أحلى
"Come on" get it from the net, goalkeeper!	hat-ha mnish-shabaka ya goal	هاتها من الشبكة يا «جول»
Let's say "congratulations" to winner and "hard luck" to loser	nguul mabruuk lil-fa'z w-hard luck lil-khas-ran	نقول مبروك للفائز و(هارد لك) للخسران
A dangerous, well-played and beautiful "kick" of a ball	koarah khaTiiiiiiiiiira w-mal3uubah w-jamiilah	كورة خطيييييرة وملعوبة وجميلة

70

The Desert — البرّ! *'il-barr!*

المعنى Meaning	Transliteraton	Word الكلمة
The desert	*'il-barr – 'iS-Sa7ra*	البر / الصحرا
All farm animals	*7alal*	حلال
Sand dune	*3arguub*	عرقوب
Sand	*ramlah*	رملة
Tent	*kheimah*	خيمة
Wood	*7iTab*	حطب
Fire	*nar – THaww*	نار – ضَو
Falcon (literally bird)	*Teir*	طير
Saluki dog	*salag – sluugi - silgan*	سلق - سلوقي – سلقان
Star	*naj-mah (pl.) nijuum*	نجمة (ج) نجوم
Moon	*gamar = gumar*	قمر
Prickle = thorn	*shoacha (pl.) shoach*	شوكة (ج) شوك
Sky	*sema*	سما
Camels and horses From the root مطيّ	*meTiy-yah*	مطيّة
Camels (racing)	*rchab*	رُكاب
Camels	*boash*	بوش
She camel	*nagah (pl.) nuug*	ناقة (ج) نوق
Baby camel	*ge3uud (pl.) gi3dan*	قعود (ج) قِعدان
Manual fan	*mehaf-fah*	مِهفّة
Woven mat	*7eStir - smaT*	حصير - سْماط
Coffee pot	*dal-lat g-hawah*	دلة قهوة
Vehicle (motor)	*say-yarah - moatar*	سيارة – موتر
Sun	*shams*	شمس
Tree	*'ish-ya-rah (pl.)* *shayar*	شجرة (ج) شجر

| Valley | *wadii (pl.) widyan* | وادي (ج) وديان |
| Oasis | *wa7ah (pl.) wa7at* | واحة (ج) واحات |

More about ʻil-barr

People tend to check weather condition before they go to the desert. Learn these expressions:

It is sunny (There is sun)	شي شمس *shayy shams* = فيه شمس *fiih shams*
It is cloudy	شي غيم (سحاب) *shayy gheim (se7ab)* = فيه غيم = *fiih gheim, fiih sa7ab* (سحاب)
It is windy	شي هوا *shayy huwa* = فيه هوا *fiih huwa*
It is raining	شي مطر *shayy meTar* = فيه مطر *fiih meTar*
There is a sand storm	شي عجاج *shayy 3ajaj* = فيه عجاج *fiih 3ajaj* =عاصفة رملية *3aSfah ramliy-yah*
It is foggy	شي ضباب *shayy THebab* = فيه ضباب *fiih THebab*
Thunder	رعد *ra3ad*
Lightening	برق *barg*
Weather	جو *jaww*

It is also important to know the points of the compass while being in the desert:

North	*ʻish-shemal*	الشمال
South	*ʻil-jenuub = ʻil-yenuub*	الجنوب
East	*ʻish-sharg*	الشرق
West	*ʻil-gharb*	الغرب

72

Animals — 'il-7ayawanat الحيوانات

Meaning المعنى	Transliteraton	Word الكلمة
Farm (animals)	3izbah	عزبة
Farm (agricultural)	mazra3ah	مزرعة
Camel	jaml = yamal / ba3iir	جمل / بعير
Goats	ghanam	غنم
Cows	bagar	بقر
Horse	7iSan	حصان
Mare	faras	فرس
Rooster	diik = diich	ديك
Chicken	diya-yah	دجاجة
Dog	kalb = chalb	كلب
Cat	gaTuu	قطو
Donkey	7mar	حمار
Ghazal	ghazal	غزال
Pigeon	7amamah	حمامة
Bird (sparrow)	3aSfuur	عصفور
Birds	Toyuur	طيور
Lion	'asad	أسد
Lioness	labwah	لبوة
Tiger	nimer	نمر
Elephant	fiil	فيل
Falcon	Sagir	صقر
Butterfly	farashah	فراشة
Rabbit	'arnab	أرنب
Crocodile	timsa7	تمساح
Serpent / snake	7ay-yah / 7iniish = thu3ban	حية / حنيش = ثعبان
Duck	baT-Tah	بطة
Wolf	dhiib	ذيب
Fox	tha3lab	ثعلب

73

In the Market   في السوق

Meaning المعنى	Transliteraton	Word الكلمة
How much is this?	'ib-kam hadha?	بكم هذا؟
O.K., why is it expensive?	Tay-yib leish ghalii?	طيب، ليش غالي؟
Give us a break! (price)	ra3iina shwayy	راعينا شوي
What's the bottom price?	kamm 'aakhir?	كم آخر؟
By God! this is what it cost me	ras malha wAllah!	راس مالها والله!
At my expense	3ala 7sabi	على حسابي
By God! It is cheap	w-Allah rekhiiS	والله رخيص!
Free of charge	maj-janan = 'ib-balash	مجانًا = بلاش
That's it! I do not want to buy	khalaS maba 'ashtirii	خلاص مايا أشتري
I do not like it	ma 3e-ybnii	ما عجبني
Do you have change?	3indik khardah?	عندك خُردة؟
Let me pay for it	khalii 3aleina	خلي علينا
Do you have sweets?	3indek 7alawiy-yat?	عندك حلويات؟
Special offer	3arTH khaS	عرض خاص
Where is the bakery? Baker	wein l- makhbaz? 'il-khab-baz?	وين المخبز؟ الخباز؟

74

Fruits and Vegetables

Meaning المعنى	Transliteraton	Word الكلمة
Fruits فاكهة		
Mango	manga = hamba	منجا = همبا
Pear	kem-mathra	كمثرى
Pineapple	'ananas	أناناس
Pomegranate	rem-man	رمّان
Raspberry	tuut	توت
Strawberry	farawlah	فراولة
Dates (different stages)	tamr = si77	تمر = سح
Apple	tif-fa7	تفاح
Orange	birtiqal	برتقال
Tangerine	SanTara	سنطرة
Chestnut	kastana = bu farwa	كستنا = بو فروة
Sweet Potato	findal	فندال
Truffle	fage3	فقع
Watermelon	yi77	جح
Grape	3inab	عنب
Banana	moaz	موز
Apricot	mishmish	مشمش
Plum	khoakh	خوخ
Vegetables خضرة		
Cauliflower	zahra	زهرة
Cucumber	khyar	خيار
Ginger	zanjebiil	زنجبيل
Hot pepper	filfil	فلفل
Lettuce	khass	خس
Onions	beSal	بصل
Parsley	baqduunis	بقدونس

75

Radish	*fijil*	فجل
Eggplant	*beidhiyan*	بيذيان
Potato	*beTaT*	بطاط
Cabbage	*malfuuf*	سلفوف
Olive	*zaytuun*	زيتون
Carrot	*yizar*	جزر
Garlic	*thuum*	ثوم
Zuccine	*kuusa*	كوسا

Food Features — صفات الأكل

Meaning المعنى	Transliteraton	Word الكلمة
Delicious	*zein*	زين = غاوي
Hot	*7arr*	حار
Spicy	*yi7rig*	يحرق حار
Cold	*barid*	بارد
Salty	*mali7*	مالح
Sour	*7amiTH*	حامض
Bitter	*morr*	مرّ
Leftover	*mbay-yit*	مبيّت
Fresh	*Tazij*	طازج
Tasteless	*maSikh*	ماصخ
Sweet	*7elu /7alii*	حلو / حالي

Meals   'il-wajbat الوجبات

المعنى Meaning	Transliteraton	الكلمة Word
Breakfast Note: Breakfast in remTHan is *feTuur*	*feTuur / ryuug*	فطور / ريوق
Lunch	*gheda*	غدا
Dinner	*3esha*	عشا
Guests' snacks	*fuwalah*	فوالة
Invitation for meal – any occasion	*3eziimah*	عزيمة

أفعال شايعة عن الوجبات

Common Verbs About Meals

المعنى Meaning	Transliteraton	الكلمة Word
Take breakfast	*fiTar, yfTar* *tray-yag, ytray-yag*	فطر، يفطر تريّق، يتريّق
Take lunch	*tghad-da, yetghad-dah*	تغدى - يتغدّى
Take dinner	*t3ash-sha, yet3ash-sha*	تعشّى - يتعشّى
Take coffee	*tgahwa, yetgahwa*	تقهوى - يتقهوى
Pour	*Sebb, ySibb*	صب - يصبّ
Serve (Food)	*nichab, ynchib*	نكب - ينكب

77

Meaning المعنى	Transliteraton	Word الكلمة
Main dish, brown rice with fish or meat	*mechbuus*	مكبوس
Main dish, rice with meat, chicken or fish mixed with special spices	*bir-yanii*	برياني
Smashed wheat, chicken or meat mixed with spices	*hiriis*	هريس
Main dish: meat or chicken with vegetables	*thiriid*	ثريد
Red stew of chicken, meat or fish	*Saloanah*	صالونة
Main dish: lamb meat with bread and rice	*ghuuzii*	غوزي
Appetizer: bread with honey and sesame	*khimiir*	خمير
Appetizer: boiled chickpeas	*nakhii*	نخي
Appetizer: Emirati pancake with honey	*chibab*	تشباب
Pasta, oil, sugar and saffaron (comes with fried eggs at the top)	*balaliiT*	بلاليط
Thin flakes of bread	*khibz 'ir-regag*	خبز رقاق
Appetizer: boiled brown beans	*bajila*	باجلا
Smashed rice, chicken or mean, onion, tomato, garlic and Emirati spices	*maTHruuba*	مضروبة
Main dish: smashed sharks with bread or rice	*jishiid*	جشيد
Main dish: boiled salted fish with spices	*mali7*	مالح
Fresh fried fish spawn	*'i7buul*	حبول

Emirati Deserts — الحلويات الإماراتية

Meaning المعنى	Transliteraton	Word الكلمة
Mixed flour, egg, saffaron and cardamom (all fried in oil and served with dates syrup)	*ligeimat / geimat*	لقيمات / قيمات
Cereals, sugar and saffaron	*sagaw*	ساقو
Flour, sugar, oil, rose water and cardamom	*khebiiS*	خبيص
Dates with sauce	*bithiith*	بثيث

Micillaneous (Dishes and drinks)

Meaning المعنى	Transliteraton	الكلمة Word
Chicken	diyay	دجاج
Meat	le7em	لحم
Fish	simach	سمك
Shrimp	robiyan	روبيان
Salad	salaTah	سلطة
Cheese	jibn	جبن
Salt	mil7	ملح
Sugar	shekar	سكر
Vegetables	khiTHrah	خضرة
Fruits	fawakih	فواكه
Sweets	7alawah	حلاوة
Yougurt	roab	روب
Rice	3eish	عيش
Bread	khibz	خبز
Chocolate	kakaw	كاكاو
Thyme, zatar	za3tar	زعتر
Tea (cooked with milk)	karak	كرك
Read cereals, saffaron,, carda-mom, custor and milk	'il7abea l-7amrah	الحبة الحمرا
Tea	chai	شاي
Water	mai	ماي
Coffee	gahwah	قهوة

Clothes 'il-malabis الملابس

Meaning المعنى	Transliteraton	Word الكلمة
Long garment for men	kandoarah	كندورة
A white hat comes under headscarf (men)	ga7-fiy-yah	قحفية
Long black dress (women)	3abayah	عباية
Suit	badla	بدلة
Dress	fistan	فستان
Pants	banTaloan	بنطلون
Shirt	qamiiS	قميص
Koufiya	ghitra	غترة
Socks	dlagh / zlagh	دلاغ / زلاغ
Shoes, Sandals	n3al	نعال
Sneakers	juuti	جوتي
Scarf (for women)	sheilah	شيله
Kilt – Traditional men's under-garment	wzar	وزار
Men's undergarment shirt	faniilah	فانيله
Underpants	sirwal	سروال
Men's cloak	bisht	بشت

Colors   'il-'alwan الألوان

Meaning	Plural		Feminine singular		Masculine singular	
White	*biiTH*	بيض	*beiTHa*	بيضا	*'abyaTH*	أبيض
Black	*suud*	سود	*soada*	سودا	*'aswad*	أسوَد
Blue	*zirg*	زرق	*zarga*	زرقا	*'azrag*	أزرق
Red	*7omr*	حمر	*7amra*	حمرا	*'a7mar*	أحمر
Green	*khoTHr*	خضر	*khaTHra*	خضرا	*'akhTHar*	أخضر
Yellow	*Sofer*	صفر	*Safra*	صفرا	*'aSfar*	أصفر
Brown	*bin-niy-yh* *bin-niy-yat*	بنية بنيّات	*bin-niy-yah*	بنية	*bin-ni*	بني
Gray	*remadiy-yah* *remadiy-yat*	رمادية رماديّات	*remadiy-yah*	رمادية	*remadi*	رمادي
Orange	*bertoqaliy-yah* *bertoqaliy-yat*	برتقالية برتقاليات	*bertoqaliy-yah*	برتقالية	*bertqalii*	برتقالي
Tan	*somr*	سمر	*samra*	سمرا	*'asmar*	أسمر
Blonde	*shogr*	شقر	*shagra*	شقرا	*'ashgar*	أشقر
Navy blue	*ki7liy-yah* *ki7liy -yat*	كحلية كحليات	*ki7liy-yah*	كحلية	*ki7lii*	كحلى

متلوّن *mitlaw-win*

In Arabic, you can describe someone who is very changeable by saying that the person is "changeable in color", meaning that this person is sneaky and has many moods and unpredictable conditions.

له ألف لون ولون

lah 'alf loan w loan

He has a thousand colors

فلان كل يوم له لون

flan kil yoam lah loan

So and so has a color for each day

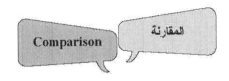

Comparison — المقارنة

Superlatives can be formed from simple adjectives such جميل،
طويل، زين by adding initial *alif* + the root. Note the following:

Beautiful ------ more beautiful	*jamiil* ------ *'ajmal*	جميل ------ أجمل
Tall ------ taller	*Tuwiil* ------ *'aTwal*	طويل ------ أطْوَل
Pretty ------ prettier	*zein* ------ *'azyan*	زين ------ أزْين
High ------ higher	*3alii* ------ *'a3la*	عالي-------أعلى
Sweet ------ sweeter	*7ilo* ------ *'a7la*	حلو ------ أحلى
Hot ------ hotter	*7arr* ------ *'a7arr*	حارّ ------ أحرّ

The Superlatives:

1- Superlatives may be formed by using the comparative form followed by an indefinite noun. Example:

The prettiest girl	*'ajmal bint*	أجمل بنت
The most rational boy	*'a3gal walad*	أعقل ولد
The simplest thing	*'absaT shayy*	أبيسط شي

When comparing two things, we use the preposition من *min* "than, from".
Example:

| Al-Anoud is taller than Khulood. | *'il3enuud 'aTwal min khuluud.* | العنود أطول من خلود |
| Hamad is older than Sultan. | *7amad 'akbar min SelTan.* | حمد أكبر من سلطان |

Note the following:

Hot ------ hotter	*7ar-ran ----7ar-ran 'akthar*	حران-------- حران أكثر
Tired ------ more tired	*ta3ban----- ta3ban 'akthar*	تعبان --------- تعبان أكثر
Cold ------ colder	*bardan----- bardan 'akthar*	بردان ------- بردان أكثر

Home Furniture, Bathroom and Kitchen Equipments

Furniture	'athath		أثاث
Bathroom	7am-mam		حمام
Kitchen	maTbakh		مطبخ

المعنى بالانجليزية English Meaning	Plural الجمع		Singular المفرد	
Bed	shebarii	شباري	shibriy-yah	شبرية
Pillow	muwasid	موامد	muusedah	موسدة
Quilt	l7fah	لحفة	l7af	لحاف
Sheets	gheTya	غطية	gheTa	غطا
Cover	farsh	فرش	farsh	فرش
Mattress	duwashig	دواشق	doashag	دوشق
Cabinet / Wardrobe	kabatat	كبتات	kabat	كبت
Table	Tawalat	طاولات	Tawlah	طاولة
Fan	marawi7	مراوح	merwa7ah	مروحة
Curtain	sitayir	ستاير	setarah	ستارة
Sofa	kanabat	كنبات	kanab	كنب
Chair	karasi	كراسي	kirsii	كرسي
Rug	zuwalii zill	زوالي زل	zuuliy-yah	زولية
Light	leitat	ليتات	leit	ليت
Television	telfezyoanat	تلفزيونات	telfezyoan	تلفزيون
Radio	raduw-wat radioat	رادوّات راديوات	radio radu	راديو رادو
Recorder	msaj-jilat	مسجلات	msaj-jil	مسجل
Fridge	thal-lajat	ثلاجات	thal-lajah	ثلاجة

85

Washing machine	ghas-salat	غسالات	ghas-salah	غسالة
Dryer	nash-shafat	نشافات	nash-shafah	نشافة
Plate	S7uun	صحون	Sa7en	صحن
Spoon	gefash	قفش	gafshah	قفشة
	khuwashiig	خواشيق	khashuuga	خاشوقة
Fork	shu-wak	شوك	shoakah	شوكة
Knife	sichachiin	سكاكين	sichiin	سكين
Glass	glaSat	قلاصات	glaS	قلاص
Jug	jeikat	جيكات	jeik	جيك
	debab	دبب	dab-bah	دبّة
Bowl	mlal	ملال	mallah	ملّة
Tray	Suwani	صواني	Siiniy-yah	صينية
Traditional table cloth for food made of fronds to be used on the floor for eating	sarariid	سراريد	sar-ruud	سرّود
Coffee cup	fanayiin	فناجين	finyan	فنجان
Oven	'afran	أفران	firn	فرن
Trash bin			zibalah	زبالة

Verbs Used With Furniture

انكلمة Word	Transliteraton	المعنى Meaning
Sleep	*nam = regad*	نام = رقد
Cover	*ghaT-Ta*	غطى
Wrapp him / herself	*tla7-7af*	تلحف
Sit on	*ge3ad 3ala = yilas 3ala*	قعد على = جلس على
Burn	*'i7terag*	احترق
Light up / ignite	*wal-la3*	ولّع
Switch on	*shagh-ghal*	شغّل
Switch off	*ban-ned*	بنّد
Close	*sak-kar*	سكّر
Spread	*ferash*	فرش
Wash	*ghesal*	غِسَل

Meaning المعنى	Transliteraton	Word الكلمة
Real estate employee	mo-waTH-THaff 3aqarat	موظف عقارات
Apartment	shaq-qah	شقة
Building	3emarah	عمارة
	benayah	بناية
Floor	doar	دور
Hall	Salah	صالة
Rent	'iijar	إيجار
In advance	muqad-daman	مقدمًا
Villa	veil-la	فيلا
Swimming pool	masba7	مسبح

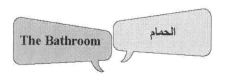

The Bathroom — الحمام

الكلمة Word	Transliteraton	المعنى Meaning
Sink	meghsalah	مغسلة
Bathtub	ban-yo	بانيو
	7oaTH	حوض
Siphon	siifoan	سيفون
Brush	firshat	فرشاة
Tooth brush	firshat 'asnan	فرشاة أسنان
	bruush	بروش
Tooth paste	ma3juun 'asnan	معجون أسنان
Hair brush	firshat sha3ar	فرشاة شعر
Comb	mishT	مِشط
Shaving brush	firshat 7lagah	فرشاة حلاقة
Shaving blade, Razor	muus 7lagah	موس حلاقة
Water and sope	may w Sabuun	ماي وصابون
Faucet	7anafiy-yah / Sanbuur	حنفية / صنبور
laundry	ghesiil	غسيل
Scissors	megaSS	مقص
Towel	fuuTah	فوطة
	fuudah	فودة

Verbs Related to Bathroom

Wash	ghas-sal		غَسَّل
Bathe	seba7		سبَح
Comb	mash-shaT		مَشَّط
Comb	sa7-7a		سَحَّى
Shave	7al-lag		حَلَّق
Dry	nash-shaf		نَشَّف

90

المعنى Meaning	Transliteraton	الكلمة Word
Street	shari3	شارع
Sidewalk	raSiif	رصيف
Roundabout	daw-war	دوار
Entrance	madkhal	مدخل
Exit	makhraj	مخرج
Turn	laf-fah	لفة
Signal	'isharah	إشارة
Bridge	jisr	جسر
Area	minTaqah	منطقة
Tunnel	nafaq	نفق
Lane	masar	مسار
Distance	masafah	مسافة
Intersection	taqato3	تقاطع
Police	sherTah	شرطة
Violation, fine	mokhalafah	مخالفة
Accident	7adith	حادث
Too crowded	wayid za7mah	واجد زحمة
Map	khariiTa	خريطة
Post office	maktab bariid	مكتب بريد
Bank	bank	بنك
Port	miina	ميناء
Garden / Park	7adiiqa	حديقة
Cooperation Society	jam3iy-ya ta3awuniy-ya	جمعية تعاونية
Police station	markaz sherTa	مركز شرطة
Mall	markaz tijari = moal	مركز تجاري = مول
Company	sharikah	شركة
Pharmacy	Sai-daliy-yah	صيدلية
Firm / foundation	mo'as-sasah	مؤسسة

Institution	ma3-had	معهد
shop	ma7al	محل
Shop	dek-kan	دكان
Museum	mat7af	متحف
Gas station	shiishat betroal	شيشة بترول
Bus station	ma7aTat baS	محطة باص
Hospital	mustashfa	مستشفى
Embassy	safarah	سفارة
Building	binayah	بناية
Mosque	mas-yed = jami3	مسجد = جامع
Church	kaniisah	كنيسة
University	jam3ah	جامعة
College	kil-liyah	كلية
Airport	maTar	مطار
Neighborhood	feriij	فريج
Area	minteqah	منطقة
Graveyard	magbarah	مقبرة
Municipality	baladiy-yah	بلدية
Court	meh-kemah	محكمة
Hotel	fundoq	فندق
Village	qar-yah	قرية
City	mediinah	مدينة
Island	jaziirah	جزيرة
Capital	3aSimah	عاصمة
Exhibition	me3reTH	معرض
Authority	hai'ah	هيئة
Ministry	wizarah	وزارة
Global Village	'al-qariyah l-3alamiy-yah	القرية العالمية
Health Authority	hai'at 'iS-Si7a	هيئة الصحة
Media City	madiinat 'il-'i3lam	مدينة الإعلام
Private Sector	qiTa3 khaS	قطاع خاص
Govt. Sector	qiTa3 7ukuumii	قطاع حكومي
Ministry of Education	wizarat 'itarbiy-yah	وزارة التربية
Ministry of Health	wizarat 'iS-Si7a	وزارة الصحة

Ministry of Labor	wizarat 'il-3amal	وزارة العمل
Ministry of Foreign Affairs	wizarat 'il-kharijiy-yah	وزارة الخارجية
Ministry of Interior	wizarat 'id-dakhiliy-yah	وزارة الداخلية

How to tell someone where a place is:

Meaning المعنى	Transliteraton	Word الكلمة
Go straight	ruu7 siida	روح سيدا
Turn right	liff yemiin	لف يمين
Take the first / second / third left	khedh 'aw-wal / thani / thalith yesar	خذ أول / ثاني / ثالث يسار
First / second street on the left / the right	'aw-wal / thani shari3 3ala 'il-yasar/ 'il-yemiin	أول / ثاني شارع على اليسار / اليمين
The market is on the left / right / straight	'is-suug 3ala 'il-yasar / 'il-yemiin / siida	السوق على اليسار/ اليمين / سيدا
Go past the mosque	Tuuf 'il-mesyid	طوف المسجد
It is close to / far from here	huu geriib min / be3iid 3an hnii	هو قريب من / بعيد عن هني
It is twenty minutes from here	hiyy 3ishriin degiigah min hnii	هي عشرين دقيقة من هني
Before the university	gabil 'il-jam3ah	قبل الجامعة
After the university	ba3d = (3ugub)-'il jam3ah	بعد = (عقب) الجامعة
Beside the palace	3ind 'il-gaSir	عند القصر
Beside the harbor	yamm 'il-miina	جنب المينا

93

استعمالات حروف الجر
وأكثر

Usage of Prepositions
and Beyond

من وين ، من هني ، من هناك

It is common to put the preposition *min* before

وين ، هني ، هناك

When asking or given directions

From where	*min wein*	من وين
From here	*min hni*	من هني
From there	*min hnak = minnak*	من هناك = مَنّاك

Remember these Expressions of Place:

In	*fii*	في
On	*3ala*	على
Under	*ta7t*	تحت
Above	*foag*	فوق
Behind	*wara*	ورا
Opposite	*mgabil*	مقابل
In front of	*jid-dam*	قدّام
Next to / beside	*yanb / yamm*	جنب
Far from	*ba3iid 3an*	بعيد عن
Close to	*gariib min*	قريب من

94

Learn these common phrases with the different expressions of place:

	fii	في
What's the matter with you? "masc. sing."	*shfiik?*	شفيك؟
	foug	فوق
More than a hundred people came	*ya foag l-'imyat nefar*	جا فوق الامية نفر
I want the upper one	*'aba 'illi foag*	أبا اللي فوق
	3ala	على
Living humbly, In accordance to capability	*3ala gad 'il-7al*	على قد الحال
As you wish, Do as you wish, goes well with your taste	*3ala keifek*	على كيفك
Why should I care about him?	*sh3alai min-na*	شعلي منه؟
He will die for a penny (very stingy)	*ymuut 3ala 'il-fils*	يموت على فلس
I am in debt!	*3alayy dyuun*	عليّ ديون
Never mind the teacher!	*ma 3leina min-l-'istadh*	ما علينا من الأستاذ
	ta7at	تحت
These problems are caused by you	*hadhi-'il-meshakil min ta7at rasek*	هذي المشاكل من تحت راسك
From below	*min ta7at*	من تحت
Under my control	*ta7at 'iidi*	تحت إيدي
	wara	ورا
Backward	*3ala wara*	على ورا
From behind, source of trouble	*min wara*	من ورا
You are the source of all troubles!	*kill-l meshaakil min warak*	كل المشاكل من وراك
Do not site in the back, Come and sir in front!	*la tiilis wara ta3al 'iilis jid-dam*	لا تجلس ورا ، تعال اجلس قدام

	ma3	مع
You are right	*ma3ak 7agg*	معاك حق
Unluckily	*ma3 l-'asaf*	مع الأسف
In spite of this, Nevertheless	*ma3 hadha*	مع هذا
	min	من
Since that day	*min dhak l-yoam*	من ذاك اليوم
I've been waiting for you for a long time	*min zaman w-'ana 'anteTHrik*	من زمان وأنا أنتظرك
From now on	*min-l-yoam w rayi7*	من اليوم ورايح
This is all because of you, This is all your fault	*kil-lah min-nek*	كله منك
I've seen you before, haven't I?	*shiftek min gabl, Sa7?*	شفتك من قبل، صح؟
When he sings, everyone listens	*min yghan-ni 'il-kill yisma3*	من يغني الكل يسمع
I entered from the window	*dash-sheit min 'id-deriishah*	دشيت من الدريشة
From the beginning	*min-l 'aw-wal*	من الأول

Word الكلمة	Transliteraton	Meaning المعنى
I want to open an account	'aba 'afta7 7isab	أبا أفتح حساب
Current account	7isab jarii	حساب جاري
Saving ccount	7isab tawfiir	حساب توفير
Our dear agent (customer)	3amiilona-l-3aziiz	عميلنا العزيز
Investment	'istithmar	استثمار
Profit	fai-dah	فايدة
Loan	qarTH	قرض
Salary	ratib	راتب
Deposit	'iida3	ايداع
There is no balance (funds)	ma fii raSiid	ما في رصيد!
Fixed deposit	wedii3ah	وديعة
Credit card	kart 'i'timan	كرت انتمان

Meaning المعنى	Transliteraton	Word الكلمة
Open	*maftuu7*	مفتوح
Closed	*magfuul*	مقفول
	mask-kar	مسكّر
Closed for prayer	*mask-kar liS-Salah*	مسكر للصلاة
Made of gold	*maSnuu3 min dhahab*	مصنوع من ذهب
Made of silver	*maSnuu3 min fiTH-THah*	مصنوع من فضة
Made of silk	*maSnuu3 min 7eriir*	مصنوع من حرير
Made of cotton	*maSnuu3 min geTen*	مصنوع من قطن
Made of wool	*maSnuu3 min Suuf*	مصنوع من صوف
Rug	*siy-yadah / siyayiid* (pl.)	سجادة / سجاجيد
Coffee pot	*dal-lah / dlal* (pl.)	دلة / دلال
Customer	*zebuun / zeba-yin* (pl.)	زبون / زباين
Seller	*bay-ya3 / bay-ya3iin* (pl.)	بياع / بياعين
Shop owner	*ra3i dik-kan*	راعي دكان
Earings	*7alag / 7elgan* (pl.)	خلق / حلقان
Long earings	*shghab / shghabat* (pl.)	شغاب / شغابات
Khol pot	*mik7ala / mika7il* (pl.)	مكحلة / مكاحل
Pot	*jidr / jduur* (pl.)	قدر / قدور
Necklace, chain	*silselah / salasil* (pl.)	سلسلة / سلاسل
Clay	*fakh-khar*	فخار
Jewelry box (used for other storage purposes)	*manduus / menadiis* (pl.)	مندوس / مناديس

Word الكلمة	Transliteraton	Meaning المعنى
Student (male) / student (female)	*Talib / Talibah*	طالب / طالبة
School	*madrasah*	مدرسة
Book	*kitab*	كتاب
Notebook	*daftar*	دفتر
Page	*Saf7ah*	صفحة
Lesson	*dars*	درس
Pen	*galam*	قلم
Class	*Saff*	صف
Supervisor	*mushrif / mu-waj-jih*	مشرف / موجه
School uniform	*zii madrasii*	زيّ مدرسي
Holiday	*'ijazah / 3oTlah*	إجازة / عطلة

99

Common Words   كلمات شائعة

Word الكلمة	Transliteraton	Meaning المعنى
Probably	'i7timal	احتمال
Eat "sing. masc. imp."	kill	كل
Yesterday	'ams	أمس
Certainly	'akiid	أكيد
Call "sing. masc. imp."	'it-tiSl	اتصّل
Now	'al7iin	الحين
Tomorrow	bachir	باكر
Go away! "imp. masc. sing."	'ingili3	انقلع
Get ready "imp. masc. sing."	'ista-3id	استعد
Enough, but	bas	بس
Outside # inside	bar-rah # da-khil	برّه # داخل
Later, afterwards, then	ba3dein	بعدين
Without	biduun	بدون
Ready	jahiz = zahib	جاهز = زاهب
Coming	yai	جاي
Sitting	yalis	جالس
Similar, like, same as	sherat	شرات
Correct	Sa7	صح
Wrong	ghalaT	غلط
Amazing	3ajiib	عجيب
Loser	fashil	فاشل
Place	mekan	مكان
Intending	nawii	ناوي
Let's, hurry	yal-lah	يلّا
O.K.	'inzein	انزين
Old	mal 'aw-wal	مال أول

Thing	shayy	شي
Gift	hadiy-yeh	هدية
Thing, (pl.) stuff	gharaTH (pl.) 'aghraTH	غرض (ج) أغراض
Picture, image	Suurah	صورة
Old # new	jidiim # yidiid	قديم # جديد
Important	mehimm	مهم
Necessary	THaruuri	ضروري
Type, kind	noa3	نوع
Individual (human)	'insan	إنسان
One (person)	7add	حدّ
No one	ma7add	محد
People	nas	ناس
What's the reason?	shu 'is-sabab?	شو السبب؟
Newspaper	jariidah	جريدة
Life	7ayah	حياة
Death	moat	موت
Order (N.)	niTHam	نظام
Law	qanuun	قانون
Bill	fatuura	فاتورة
Electricity	kahrabah	كهربا
Danger	khaTar	خطر
Song	'ughniyah	أغنية
Music	muusiiqa	موسيقى
Nonsense	maS-kharah	مصخرة
Art	fann	فن
Joke	nuktah	نكتة
Yes	heih	هيه
No	la	لا
Available, present	maw-juud	موجود
Dialect	lahjah	لهجة
Language	lughah	لغة
Idea	fikrah	فكرة
Mine (belongs to me)	malii	مالي
Not mine	mob malii	مب مالي

101

By myself	'ibruu7ii	بروحي
Always	doam	دوم
Once, one time	mar-rah	مرة
Twice	mar-tein	مرتين
Sometimes, times	mar-rat	مرات
Or	'aw / wal-la	أو / ولا
Little	jiliil	قليل
Much, a lot	kithiir	كثير
Rare	nader	نادر
Impossible	musta7iil	مستحيل
If	'idha	إذا
Suitable	munasib	مناسب
Not suitable	mob munasib	مب مناسب
O.K., alright	mashii	ماشي
Busy, occupied	mob faTHii	مب فاضي
Hard	Sa3b	صعب
Easy	sahl	سهل
Choice	'ikhti-yar	اختيار
With	ma3 / wiy-ya	مع / ويّا
Destiney, share	naSiib	نصيب
A lot	wayid	واجد
Stay in... (remain in...)	khal-liik fii...	خليك في...
Severe pressure	THaghT shediid	ضغط شديد

المعنى Meaning	Transliteraton	الكلمة Word
God knows best	*Allah 'a3lam*	الله أعلم
You are super!	*'inta dhahab!*	إنت ذهب!
I need action	*'aba fi3l*	أبا فعل
May God heal you (also used ironically when someone misbehaves).	*Allah yshfiik*	الله يشفيك
I'm at your service	*'int tamer*	إنت تامر
It seems that	*'iTH-THahir 'in-nah*	الظاهر إن
Shame!	*'afa 3aleik*	أفا عليك
God willing	*inshaAllah*	إن شا الله
May God protect us.	*Allah bis'sitir*	الله بالستر
Either … or	*'im-ma 'aw*	إما ... أو
May God protect you / I beg you.	*Allah ykhal-liik*	الله يخليك
Let's hope so. (Literally, "God is generous.")	*Allah kariim*	الله كريم
May God bless you. (Reply to: مبروك)	*Allah ybarik fiik*	الله يبارك فيك
To hell with + pronoun	*'inshaAllah 3ann +* pronoun	إن شا الله عن
Please, I beg you	*'arjuuk*	أرجوك
Fast worker, quick thief (Literally, "His hand is light.")	*'iiduh khafii-feh*	إيده خفيفة
As soon as	*'aw-wal ma*	أول ما
People of your kind	*'amthal-kum*	أمثالكم
May God damn you	*Allah yil3ank*	الله يلعنك
The essence, summary, conclusion	*'il-khulaSah — 'iz-zibdeh*	الخلاصة — الزبدة

103

Be sure you do not…	'iy-yak	إياك
Unless	'il-la 'idha	إلا إذا
Oh, let me tell you	'aguul lek	أقول لك
Wait a little	'uSbor shwayy	اصبر شوي
May God honor you!	'akramkom Allah	أكرمكم الله
I am with a group of people	'ana wiy-ya jema3a	أنا ويا جماعة
Goodbye	brekhSetkum	برخصتكم
What's wrong?	belak? = shbelak	بلاك؟ = شبلاك
It is still…	ba3deh	بعده
Girl / lady from a wealthy family (Literally, "Daughter of blessings.")	bint ni3meh	بنت نعمة
Quickly	bsor3ah	بسرعة
With difficulty	bsu3uubah	بصعوبة
Easily	bsihuulah	بسهولة
Without a reason	biduun sebab	بدون سبب
Decent girl	bint 7alal	بنت حلال
For God's sake	bil-lah 3aleik	بالله عليك
Without	biduun ma	بدون ما
Instead of	bedal ma	بدل ما
No need	belash	بلاش
For free	bebelash – 'b-belash	ببلاش – بَلاش
In good faith	be7esin niy-yah	بحسن نية
Country with abundance	bilad kheir	بلاد خير
In any way, in any form	bi-'ayy shekl	بأي شكل
Frankly	biSara7ah	بصراحة
Done!, you got it!	tamm	تم!
Wait a little	tray-yah shwayy	ترّيا شوي
May you come back safely (sing. masc.)	tridd bis-salamah	تردّ بالسلامة
Or else, by God I will…	tara wa-Allah	ترى والله
Excuse me for the expression / word	tikram	تكرم
You deserve it! (positive and negative)	tistahil	تستاهل

Under my control	te7t 'iidii	تحت ايدي
I have just	taw-wnii	توني
Keep in mind	7oT fii balak	حط في بالك
Used for greeting someone (Welcome!)	7ay-yaka Allah	حيّاك الله
It / he drove me nuts!	khab-bal bii!	خبّل بي!
Hope it's all good	kheir 'inshaAllah	خير إن شا الله
Simple minded	khefiif 3agil	خفيف عقل
I am concerned for you.	khoafii 3aleik	خوفي عليك
Let me pay for it!	khallii 3aleina	خلّه علينا
Held a grudge	khidh b-khaTerh	خذ بخاطره
It's bad already	kharbanah ... khar-banah	خربانة... خربانة
Be a man!	khal-lak ray-yal	خلّك رجال
The gist, the summary of the issue	khulaSat 'il-mau-THuu3 = 'il-khu-laSah= khulaSat 'is-salfah	خلاصة الموضوع! = الخلاصة =خلاصة السالفة
Round-trip	roa7ah red-dah	روحة وردّة
Send regards to	sal-lim 3ala	سلّم على
Send my regards to your brother. sal-lim (to man), sal-lmii (to woman)	sal-lim 3ala-khuuk	سلّم على أخوك
Send my regards to your mother "fem. sing."	sal-lmii 3al-walda	سلمي عالوالدة
God protect you! "Said to a masc. sing." sallamka Allah (to man), sallamchi Allah (to woman)	sal-lamk Allah	سلّمك الله!

English	Transliteration	Arabic
Thank you!	*tislam*	تسلم
And he who says	response: *w min gal salim*	ومن قال سالم
	response: *w min gal*	ومن قال
The year that	*senat ma*	سنة ما
Cardiac arrest	*sekta galbiy-yah*	سكتة قلبية
He did the impossible	*sew-wah l-mosta7iil*	سوى المستحيل
What happened?	*shuu 'illi jera?*	شو اللي جرى؟
	sh-Sar?	شصار؟
	shu 'istewa?	شو استوى؟
What's up?	*sh-salfah?*	شالسالفة؟
This is natural	*shayy Tabii3ii*	شي طبيعي
Personally	*shakhSiy-yan*	شخصيًا
What is this foolishness?	*shuu-hal-maS-kharah?*	شو هالمصخرة؟
Why should I care about him?	*sh3alai min-nah?*	شعليَ منه؟
"Come our way" (said to grab someone's attention)	*Soabna!*	صوبنا!
Correct or incorrect?	*Sa7 wal-la la?*	صح ولّا لا؟
Patient	*Tuwill bal*	طويل بال
Patient	*Tuwiil rou7*	طويل روح
May you live a long life. (Expression of respect)	*Tal 3emrek*	طال عمرك
I had high expectation of	*3esh-shamt nafsii*	عشّمت نفسي
To the peak	*3al-'aakhir*	ع الأخر
I have never	*3emrii ma*	عمري ما
In reality	*3aT-Tabii3ah*	ع الطبيعة
I thought…	*3ala balii / 3a-balii*	على بالي / ع بالي
Flirty, looks at girls	*3iyuu-neh Tuwiilah*	عيونه طويلة
Over my dead body	*3ala jith-thitii*	على جثّتي
Special offer	*3arTH khaS*	عرض خاص
On the left	*3al yesar*	عاليسار
When needed, in case of need	*3ind-l-lizuum*	عند اللزوم

As the proverb goes	3ala goal-l-methel	على قول المثل
Give me an example	3aTnii mithal	عطني مثال
According to the way	3ala 'Tariiga	على الطريقة
Then	3iyal	عيل
I hope nothing is wrong	3esa ma sharr	عسى ما شر
Anyways, in general	3umuuman 3al-3umuum	عمومًا على العموم
Cut it short	3aTnii 'iz-zebdah	عطني الزبدة
Only for you man	3eshanak bas ya ray-yal	عشانك بس يا رجال
By force, against the will of...	ghaSban 3an...	غصبًا عن...
As soon as possible	fii 'asra3 waqt	في أسرع وقت
Impolite	jiliil-l-'adab / jiliil-l 7iya	قليل الأدب / قليل الحيا
Has the ability to put up with a lot of suffering (Literally, "a cat.")	gaTuu	قطو
I mean	gaSdii	قصدي
(You should've, why didn't you) tell me from the beginning	guul mni-l-bidayah ya 'akhii!	قول من البداية يا أخي!
Get married (Literally, "Complete the other half of your religion")	kam-mil nuS diinek	كمل نص دينك
Everyone who	kill min	كل من
Whenever	kill ma	كلما
In whatever way	keif ma	كيف ما
This is all your fault	killah minnek	كله منك
He made me sympathize with him.	kiser khaTrii	كسر خاطري
All of it together	killah 3ala ba3THah	كله على بعضه
This way and only this way. (this way or the highway)	chiih wel-la balash	كيه ولا بلاش
How dare you?	keif titjar-ra'?	كيف تتجرأ؟

So and so, Such and such	*chii w chii*	كذي وكذي
Like this, in this manner	*chidhi*	كذي
	chiih	كيه
	chidha	كذه
Don't worry	*la-tkhaf*	لا تخاف
Luckily	*li7isn-l-7eTH*	لحسن الحظ
Unluckily	*li-suu'il 7eTH*	لسوء الحظ
Until	*lein ma*	لين ما
Just for you (Literally, "for your eyes")	*le3yuunek*	لعيونك
Neither…nor	*la … w-la*	لا …ولا
Idle, doing nothing	*la sheghlah w-la meshghela*	لا شغلة ولا مشغلة
Don't (try to) fool me!	*la tgiS 3alai*	لا تقص عليّ
He got me fed up	*law-wa3 chebdii*	لوع كبدي
Do not give me a headache "masc. sing."	*la tSad-di3nii!*	لا تصدعني!
Do not be shy!	*la tisti7ii!*	لا تستحي!
I don't understand.	*mob fahim*	مب فاهم
I have no strength – I am exhausted.	*ma fiinii 7eil*	ما فيني حيل
Glory be to God	*mashaAllah*	ما شا الله
Similar to each other	*mithl ba3TH*	مثل بعض
As is	*mithl ma huu*	مثل ما هو
From the front	*min jid-dam*	من قدّام
Just as	*mithl ma*	مثل ما
Without	*min gheir ma*	من غير ما
As long as	*ma dam*	ما دام
No matter what	*meh-ma*	مهما
That is not right	*ma yeSi7*	ما يصحّ
Referring to arrogance	*min Taraf khashmeh*	من طرف خشمه
Extremely… (cold, hot, hungry, scared, tired, etc.)	*may-yit min*	ميّت من…
It is not meant to be	*ma shayy naSiib*	ما شي نصيب

No use	ma sahyy fai-dah	ما شي فايدة
You have no point	ma 3indk salfah	ما عندك سالفة
I will not interfere in your business	ma lii kheS ma lii dekhl	ما لي خص ما لي دخل
I do not have the appetite for	ma lii nefs	ما لي نفس
I am not in the mood	ma lii khilg	ما لي خلق
Too hasty, in a constant rush	mista3y-yil 3ala rizgah	مستعجل على رزقه
It is not worth it!	ma yis-wa	ما يسوى
Nothing impossible	ma fii shayy mista7iil	ما في شي مستحيل
There is nothing I can do	ma bil-yedd 7iilah	ما باليد حيلة
Even though, despite of	ma3 'in-na	مع إن...
I do not have money	ma 3indii beizat	ما عندي بيزات
I do not need to remind you of...	ma waS-Siik 3ala	ما وصيك على
Half and half, so so	niS niS	نص نص
See you later	nshuufek 3ala kheir	نشوفك على خير
Edgy	nifsah b-khashmeh	نفسه بخشمه
"Hoyamal" – sailors' chant	ho-yamal	هويامال
This is Allah's will	hadha 'amra-Allah	هاذا أمر الله
That direction, that way	haki-Soab = dhaki-Soab	هاك الصوب = ذاك الصوب
Is this a dream or reality? (I can't believe it!)	hadha 7ilm wel-la 3ilm?	هاذا حلم ولا علم؟
Nothing	wala shayy	ولا شي
How sweet you are "addressing masc. sing."	ya-7leilek "masc. sing."	يا حليلك
Dear, poor thing	ya 3emrii	يا عمري
I wish + pronoun...	ya reit	يا ريت
You are welcome (greeting and reply to thanks)	ya mer7eba	يا مرحبا
Oh God	ya Allah	يا الله

Surrender your fate to God! "masc.. sing."	*sal-lim 'amrek lil-lah!* *khal-lha 3ala-l-lah!*	سلّم أمرك لله! خلها على الله!
Response: I have trust in God	*win-ni3im bil-lah*	والنعم بالله
For your sake	*3ashan khaTrek*	عشان خاطرك
Gladly	*min 3yuuni*	من عيوني
Response: lit. means "May your eyes be healthy and safe."	Response: *tislam 3yuunek*	تسلم عيونك
As you like	*keifek, brayik* *shourek*	كيفك، برايك شورك
Good bye (said by the host to the guest)	*wda3t ir-ra7man*	وداعة الرحمن
Good bye (said by the host to the guest)	*Allah yi7faTHkum*	الله يحفظكم
Good bye (said by the host to the guest)	*fii 7ifTH ir-ra7man*	في حفظ الرحمن

Note: In Arabic, adjectives are placed after nouns. To say: "a rationale *man*" in Arabic, "*ray-yal 3agil*". To make it feminine, we add the sound "*ah*" to the end of the adjective. To say "a rationale woman" in Arabic, "*7ermah 3aglah.*"

Word الكلمة	Transliteraton	Meaning المعنى
Near	*giriib*	قريب
Far	*bi3iid*	بعيد
Tall	*tuwiil*	طويل
Short	*geSiir*	قصير
Old	*kibiir / 3oad*	كبير / عود
Clever	*dhakii*	ذكي
Stupid	*ghabii*	غبي
Generous	*kariim*	كريم
Heavy	*thijiil*	ثقيل
Light	*khefiif*	خفيف
Midium	*waSaT*	وسط
Active	*nashiiT*	نشيط
Truthful	*Sadig*	صادق
Narrow	*THay-yij*	ضيق
Baggy, wide, spacious	*wasii3*	وسيع
Weak, thin, slim	*THi3iif*	ضعيف
Honest	*'amiin*	أمين
Irresponsible	*mistahtir*	مستهتر
clean	*naTHiif*	نظيف
Filthy, dirty, bastard	*waSkh*	وسخ = وصخ
Fast	*sarii3*	سريع
Slow	*baTii'*	بطيء
Cheap	*rekhiiS*	رخيص
Expensive	*ghalii*	غالي

Coward	jaban	جبان
Amazing, fantastic (it is a noun but used as an adj.)	raw3ah	روعة
Rational	3agil	عاقل
Crazy, Dumb	khiblah = 'ahbal	خبلة = أهبل
Simple, Naiive	beSiiT	بسيط
A bad man	ray-yal ta3ban	رجال تعبان
A bad man	ray-yal rayi7 fiihaa	رجال رايح فيها
Silent, Having kept silent	mbal-lim	مبلم
Well-mannered	dharb	ذرب
Monkey!	sebal	سبال
Tired or lazy	3ayzan = met3a-yiz	عَجْزان = متعاجز
Sneaky	luuti	لوتي
Aimlessly roaming around	hayit	هايت
Well behaved, Polite	m'ad-dab	مأدب
Bum, Loafer	tambal, tanbal	تمبل = تنبل
Brave and you can rely on him	snafii	سنافي
Said to describe a brave man. Example: والنعم في عامر، أخو شما win-ni3im fi 3amer khuu sham-ma blessed 3amer for his bravery.	khuu sham-ma	خو شمّا
Liar	chadh-dhab	كذّاب
Talkative	hadhriban	هذريان
Longing for, Missing, Yearning	mishtag	مشتاق
Patient	Tuwiil ruu7	طويل روح
Amiable	khefiif ruu7	خفيف روح
Long life, Expression said to someone with great respect , e.g. father, grandfather, Sheikh	Tuwiil 'il-3emor	طويل العمر
Impolite, Rude people	geliil 'il-'adab	قليل الأدب

Unpleasant, Charming, Witty	*thegiil damm # khefiif damm*	ثقيل دم - خفيف دم
Rich	*kethiir 'il-mal*	كثير المال
Good hearted	*Tay-yib 'il-galb*	طيب القلب
Average height	*mitwaS-SiT 'iT-Tuul*	متوسط الطول
Rich, Wealthy	*maysuur 'il-7al*	ميسور الحال
Arrogant	*mitkab-bir* *khag-gag!*	متكبر خقّاق!
Very sensitive	*7as-sas*	حساس
Degraded, low, base	*min7aT*	منحط
Lucky, Fortunate	*ma7THuuTH*	محظوظ
Clever, Skillful	*shaTir*	شاطر
Elegantly dressed young man	*zgirt / zgirti*	زُقرت / زقرتي
Conscious, awake	*wa3ii*	واعي
Asleep	*ragid*	راقد
Cheater, Swindler	*ghash-shash*	غشاش
Harsh, Hard, Solid, Stiff	*gasi / jasi*	قاسي
Silent (a person being silent)	*sakit*	ساكت
Intoxicated person	*sakran*	سكران
Satisfied with someone	*raTHii*	راضي
Scared, Afraid	*kha-yif*	خايف
At fault, Mistaken	*mikh-Tii*	مخطي
Out of it (Lit: Disconnected)	*faSil*	فاصل
Stingy	*ziT-Tii*	زطّي
Imposter, swindler, cheater, crook	*mi7tal = naS-Sab*	محتال = نصّاب
Bashful, timid	*khajuul*	خجول
Reckless	*Ta-yish*	طايش
Disgusting, hideous, horrible, excellent, splendid	*faTHii3*	فظيع
In a hurry	*mista3-yil*	مستعجل

113

The following list of verbs is in the present tense. The verbs are conjugated with first person "*ana*" "I". To negate the present tense verbs, we use the word "*ma*" "not" before the verb. The following list is purposefully started with the "verb of desire" "*aba*", one can say: I want to ask "*aba 'as'al*", I want to eat "*'aba 'aakil.'* etc.

Meaning المعنى	Transliteraton	Word الكلمة
I want	'*aba* / '*ariid* / '*ab-gha*	أبا / أريد / أبغى
I need	'*a7taj*	أحتاج
I ask	'*as'al*	أسأل
I blame	'*aluum*	ألوم
I carry	'*a7mil*	أحمل
A take interest	'*ahtamm*	أهتم
I sell	'*abii3*	أبيع
I buy	'*ashtirii*	أشتري
I borrow	'*atsal-laf*	أتسلف
I cheat	'*aghish*	أغش
I arrange	'*arat-tib*	أرتب
I clean	'*anaTH-THif*	أنظف
I cut	'*agiS*	أقص
I design, I determine, decide	'*aSam-mim*	أصمم
I wipe, erase	'*amsa7*	أمسح
I draw	'*arsim*	أرسم
I choose	'*akhtar*	أختار
I breathe	'*atnaf-fas*	أتنفس
I doubt	'*ashik*	أشك
I drive	'*asuug*	أسوق
I ride	'*arkab*	أركب
I discuss	'*anaqish*	أناقش

I cheer, encourage	'ashaji3	أشجع
I compete	'anafis	أنافس
I sing	'aghan-nii	أغني
I dance	'argiS	أرقص
I finish	'akhal-liS	أخلص
I focus	'arak-kiz	أركز
I help	'asa3id	أساعد
I ignore	'aTan-nish	أطنش
I rest	'arta7	أرتاح
I get tired	'at3ab	أتعب
I give	'a3Tii	أعطي
I take	'aakidh	آخذ
I forget	'ansa	أنسى
I remember	'atdhak-kar	أتذكر
I become enemy (with)	'a3adii	أعادي
I forgive	'asami7	أسامح
I feel sleepy	'anaw-wid	أنوّد
I sleep	'argid / 'anam	أرقد / أنام
I wake up	'anish	أنش
I lay down	'ansidi7	أنسدح
I humiliate	'ahiin	أهين
I insult	'ashtim	أشتم
I invite	'a3zim	أعزم
I hate	'akrah	أكره
I learn	'at3al-lam	أتعلم
I lie	'akdhib = achdhib	أكذب
I tell the truth	'aguul 'iSara7a	أقول الصراحة
I reside, live	'askin	أسكن
I lose	'aTH-THay-yi3	أضيع
I make, do	'asaw-wii	أسوي
I watch	'aTali3	أطالع
I travel	'asafir	أسافر
I migrate	'ahajir	أهاجر
I move (from a place to another)	'antigil	أنتقل

I memorize, preserve	'a7faTH	أحفظ
I intend, mean	'agSid	أقصد
I start	'abda	أبدا
I finish	'anhii	أنهي
I repeat	'a3iid	أعيد
I return back	'araj-ji3	أرجّع
I protect	'a7mii	أحمي
I put	'a7iT	أحط
I receive	'astilim	أستلم
I send	'arsil	أرسل
I send	'aTar-rish	أطرّش
I resign	'astigiil	أستقيل
I show	'arawii	أراوي
I see	'ashuuf	أشوف
I plan	'akhaTiT	أخطط
I shave	'a7lig	أحلق
I sit	'aylis	أجلس
I smell	'ashimm	أشم
I serve	'akhdim	أخدم
I help	'asa3id	أساعد
I steal	'asrig	أسرق
I remain	'atimm	أتم
I study	'adris	أدرس
I study (for a test)	'adhakir	أذاكر
I specify	'a7ad-did	أحدد
I stand up	'awgaf	أوقف
I laugh	'aTH7ak	أضحك
I smile	'abtisim	أبتسم
I suggest	'aqtari7	أقترح
I swim	'asba7	أسبح
I take a photo	'aSaw-wir	أصوّر
I tease	'ala3wiz	ألعوز
I tie, link	'arbiT	أربط
I try	'a7awil	أحاول
I use	'astakhdim	أستخدم

I transfer	'a7aw-wil	أحوّل
I pull, withdraw (money)	'as7ab	أسحب
I push	'adiz	أدز
I wait	'atray-ya, 'antiTHir	أتريا / أنتظر
I trust	'athig	أثق
I visit	'azuur	أزور
I walk	'amshii	أمشي
I run	'arkeTH / 'arbi3	أركض / أربع
I understand	'afham	أفهم
I knock	'adigg	أدق
I fix, mend	'aSal-li7	أصلح
I complete	'akam-mil	أكمل
I build	'abnii	أبني
I apologise	'a3tidhir	أعتذر
I translate	'atarjim	أترجم
I feel	'a7is	أحس
I call	'atiS-Sil	أتصل
I chat	'asoulif	أسولف
I meet (hold a meeting)	'ajtimi3	أجتمع
I annoy, bother	'az3ij	أزعج
I smoke shisha	'asha-yish	أشيش
I smoke	'adakh-khin	أدخّن
I deserve, be worthy of	'astahil	استاهل
I talk	'armis/ 'atkal-lam	أرمس/ أتكلم
I come	'ay-yii	أجي
I try out, test	'ay-yar-rib	أجرّب
I wear, dress	'albis	ألبس
I bring	'ay-yiib	أجيب
I play	'al3ab	ألعب
I make fun of	'atT-an-naz	أتطنز
I work	'ashtighil	أشتغل
I am able to	'aruum	أروم
I throw	'a3igg	أعق
I answer, reply to someone	'aja-wib	أجاوب

I become angry	'az3al	أزعل
I become nervous	'a3aSib	أعصّب
I embarrass	'a7rij	أحرج
I deprive	'a7rim	أحرم
I eat ravenously	'ahbish	أهبش
I leave, throw away, quit, release	'ahidd	أهد
I relieve, give rest	'aray-yi7	أريح
I expect	'atwaq-qa3	أتوقع
I insist	'aS-Sirr	أصر
I donate	'atbar-ra3	أتبرع
I dream	'a7lam	أحلم
I demolish, destroy	'adam-mir	أدمّر
I lend money (to someone)	'asal-lif	أسلّف
I bargain	'afaSil, 'akasir	أفاصل، أكاسر
I postpone	'a'aj-jil	أأجّل
I provoke	'asta-fizz	استفز
I take control	'asayTir	أسيطر
I enter	'adkhil	أدخل
I leave, get out	'aTla3	أطلع
I let someone down, disappoint	'afash-shil	أفشّل
I blame (someone)	'a3atib	أعاتب
I fire, discharge (someone)	'afan-nish	أفنّش
I sponsor	'akfal	أكفل
I irritate, suppress, annoy	'ag-har	أقهر
I mix up	'akharbiT	أخربط
I open	'abaT-Til	أبطّل
I curse	'al3an	ألعن
I escape	'ahrub	أهرب
I order	'awaS-Sii 3ala	أوصّي على
I agree	'awafig	أوافق

الفعل المضارع

Simple Present

The verb أعرّف ('*a3arrif*, introduce), is formed in the present by adding certain prefixes and suffixes. Pay attention to the chart below and note the underlined suffixes and prefixes.

'*a3ar-rif*	أعرّف	'*ana* (I)	أنا
n3ar-rif	نِعرّف	*na7n* (we)	نحْن
t3ar-rif	تِعرّف	'*inta* you "masc. sing."	إنتَ
t3ar-rfiin	تِعرّفين	'*inti* you "fem. sing."	إنتِ
t3ar-rfuun	تِعرّفون	'*into* you "masc. pl."	إنتو
t3ar-rfen	تِعرفن	'*intin* you "fem. pl."	إنتن
y3ar-rif	يِعرّف	*huu* he	هو
t3ar-rif	تِعرّف	*hiya* she	هي
y3ar-rfuun	يِعرّفون	*hum* they "masc. pl."	هم
y3ar-rifen	يِعرّفن	*hinn* they "fem. pl."	هن

To negate the verb in the simple tense, we precede it with the particle ما

Negation of Simple Present نفي المضارع (الفعل أروح *'aruu 7* (I go

ma 'aruu7	ما أروح	'*ana* (I)	أنا
ma nruu7	ما نروح	*na7n* (we)	نحْن
ma truu7	ما تروح	'*inta* you "masc. sing."	إنتَ
ma truu7iin	ما تروحين	'*inti* you "fem. sing."	إنتِ
ma truu7uun	ما تروحون	'*into* you "masc. pl."	إنتو
ma truu7an	ما تروحن	'*intin* you "fem. pl."	إنتن
ma yruu7	ما يروح	*huu* he	هو
ma truu7	ما تروح	*hiya* she	هي

119

ma yruu7uun	ما يروحون	*hum* they "masc. pl."	هم
ma yruu7an	ما يروحن	*hinn* they "fem. pl."	هن

المستقبل

The Future

The future tense can be formed by adding the prefix بـ before the present tense verb and it is negated by using the word ما before the verb, connected with the prefix بـ:

I will go to the house	*baruu7 'il-beit*	بروح البيت
Will you study today?	*betidresiin 'il-yoam?*	بتدرسين اليوم؟
Are not you going to play cards?	*ma ba-til3ebuun wergah?*	ما بتلعبون ورقة؟
We will not make fun of you again	*ma benit-Tan-naz 3leik mar-ra than-ya*	ما بنطنز عليك مرة ثانية

Expressions related to future تعبيرات عن المستقبل		
Meaning المعنى	Transliteraton	Word الكلمة
Tomorrow	*bachir*	باكر
After tomorrow	*3egob bachir*	عقب باكر
Later on	*ba3dein*	بعدين
After a week / a month / a year	*3egob 'isbuu3 / shahar / senah*	عقب أسبوع / شهر / سنة
Next week	*'il-isbuu3 'il-yay*	الأسبوع الجاي
Next year	*'is-senah 'il-yaya*	السنة الجاية
In the future, God willing!	*fi-l-mustaqbal 'inshaAllah*	في المستقبل إن شاء الله

Learn the following word مترينك which means **(waiting for you)** with the different conjugations:

Meaning	Feminine مؤنث		Meaning	Masculine مذكر	
Waiting for you	mitraytin-nik	مترينّك	Waiting for you "addressing masc. sing."	mitray-yin-nik	مترّيتك
Waiting for you "fem. sing."	mitraytin-nich	مترينّك	Waiting you you "fem. sing."	mitray-yin-nich	مترينّك
Waiting for him	mitraytin-nah	مترّيتنه	Waiting for him	mitray-yin-nah	مترّيته
Waiting for her	mitraytinha	مترّيتنها	Waiting for her	mitray-yinha	مترّيتها
Waiting for them	mitraytinhum	مترّيتنهم	Waiting for them	mitray-yinhum	مترّيتنهم
Waiting for you "Pl."	mitraytinkum	مترّيتنكم	Waiting for you "Pl."	mitray-yinkum	مترّيتكم

The word توْني (I have just....) is often used before the active participle. Examples:

I've just drunk	taw-wnii sharib	توني شارب
I've just come	taw-wnii yay	توني جاي
I've just seen him	taw-wnii shayfah	توني شايفه

Past tense

الفعل "كان" بالإيجاب والنفي

The verb *kan (was)* in the affirmative and negative form

النفي Negative Form		الإيجاب Affirmative Form	
'ana maa kint, I was not	أنا ما كِنتْ	'ana kint, (I was)	أنا كِنت
'inta ma kint	إنتَ ما كِنتْ	'inta kint "you were, masc. sing."	إنتَ كِنت
'inti ma kinti	إنتي ما كِنتي	'inti kinti "you were, fem. sing."	إنتِ كِنتي
hiya ma kanat	هيْ ما كانتْ	hiya kanat "she was"	هيْ كانت
huu ma kan	هوْ ما كان	huu kan "he was"	هوْ كان
'intu ma kintu	إنتو ما كِنتو	'intu kintu "you were, masc. pl."	إنتو كنتو
na7n ma kin-na	نحن ما كّنا	ne7n kin-na "we were"	نحن كّنا
humm ma kanau	هُمْ ما كانو	humm kanau "they were, masc. pl."	هُمْ كانو
'intin ma kintin	إنتن ما كِنْتِنْ	'intin kintin "you were, fem. pl."	إنتن كنتن
hinn ma kanen	هنْ ما كانِنْ	hinn kanen "they were, fem. pl."	هِنْ كانِنْ

Imperative

المعنى بالإنجليزية Eng. Meaning	الجمع Plural (Pl.)		المفرد المؤنث Fem. Sing.		المفرد المذكر Masc. Sing.	
Renew!	yad-diduu	جددو	yad-didii	جددي	yad-did	جدّد
Study!	idrisuu	إدرسو	idrisii	ادرسي	'idris	إدرس
Put!	7iTTuu	حطو	7iTTii	حطي	7iTT	حطّ
Eat!	kiluu	كلو	kilii	كلي	kill	كل
Drink!	'ishrabuu	اشربو	'ishrebii	اشربي	'ishreb	اشرب
See!	shuufuu	شوفو	shuufii	شوفي	shuuf	شوف
Sleep!	namuu	نامو	namii	نامي	nam	نام
Bring, Fetch!	yiibuu	جيبو	yiibii	جيبي	yiib	جيب
Drink coffee!	tgahwuu	تقهوو	tgahway	تقهوي	tgah-wa	تقهوى
Promise!	'uu3iduu	اوعدو	'uu3idii	اوعدي	'uu3id	اووعد
Stop, stand!	'uugifuu	اووقفو	'uugifii	اووقفي	'uugaf	اووقف
Read!	'igruu	اقرو	'igrai	اقري	'igra	اقرا
Give	3aTuu	عطو	3aTii	عطي	3aT	عط
Shut!	Sik-kuu	صگو	Sik-kii	صگي	Sikk	صك
Come!	ta3aluu	تعالو	ta3alii	تعالي	ta3al	تعال
Go away	'injil3uu	انقلعو	'injil3ii	انقلعي	'injili3	انقلع

Open the window!	ban-nid 'ideriisha	بنّد الدريشة
Close the door!	sak-kir l-bab	سكّر الباب
Bring me coffee, please!	yiib lii gahwa, lau sime7t!	جيب لي قهوة لو سمحت!
Pour tea for me ! (get me tea!)	sebb lii shai	صب لي شاي
Help me!	sa3idnii!	ساعدني
Show me!	rawiinii	راويني
Tell me!	gill lii	قل لي

123

Demonstrative Nouns — *'asm aa' il-isharah* أسماء الإشارة

المعنى بالإنجليزية **Meaning in English**	إماراتي **Emirati**		القريب **Near object**
This "masc. sing."	*hadha*	هاذا	المذكر Masculine
This "fem. sing."	*hadhii*	هاذي	المؤنث Femenine

المعنى بالإنجليزية **Meaning in English**	إماراتي **Emirati**		البعيد **Far object**
That "masc. sing"	*hadhak* *hak*	هاذاك هاك	المذكر Masculine
That "fem. sing."	*hadhiich* *hayiich*	هاذيك هاييك	المؤنث Femenine

المعنى بالإنجليزية **Meaning in English**	إماراتي **Emirati**		المثنى والجمع **Dual and plural**
These	*hayeil* *hadhyeil*	هاييل هذيل	القريب Near object / person
Those	*hayeilak* *hadheilak*	هاييلاك هذيلاك	البعيد Far object / person

Demonstrative Adjectives

البعيد Far	القريب Near
هذاك الريال = ذاك الريال = هاك الريال *hadhak 'ir-ray-yal = dhak 'ir-ray-yal = hak ir-ray-yal*	هالريال = هاذا الريال *har-ray-yal = hadha 'ir-riy-yal*
That man	This man
هذيك الحرمة = ذيك الحرمة *hadhiich 'il-7ermah = dhiich 'il-7ermah*	هالحرمة = هاذي الحرمة *hal-7ermah = hadh-'il-7ermah*
That woman	This woman
هاييلاك الريابيل *hayeilak ir-riyayiil*	هالريابيل = هاييل الريابيل *har-riyayiil =hayeil ir-riyayiil*
Those men	These men
هاييلاك الحريم *hayeilak 'il-7eriim*	هالحريم = هاييل الحريم *hal-7eriim = hayeil 'il-7eriim*
Those women	These women

Word الكلمة	Transliteraton	Meaning المعنى
Usually	*3adatan*	عادةً
Almost	*taqriiban*	تقريبًا
Sometimes	*'a7yanan*	أحيانًا
Never	*'abdan*	أبَد = أبدًا
Personally	*shakhSiy-yan*	شخصيًا
Of course	*Tab3an*	طبعًا

نتفة *nitfah*

There is a word that is commonly used in the UAE as an expression of quantity. This word is نِتْفَة *nitfa*, which means "a bit"

I want a bit bread if you please!	*'aba nitfat khebz lau sema7t*	أبا نتفة خبز لو سمحت

Nicknames — الألقاب

Eldest Son / Daughter		'umm (mother)		buu = bu (father)	
m7ammad	محمد	umm' m7ammad	أم محمد	bu m7am-mad	بو محمد
3ashah	عائشة	umm' 3ashah	أم عائشة	bu 3ashah	بو عائشة
3abder-Ra7man	عبد الرحمن	umm' 3abder-ra7man	أم عبد الرحمن	bu 3abder-ra7man	بو عبد الرحمن

Interestingly, this does not only apply to married men and women, but also to younger people. Similar nicknames for certain names have developed over the time in relation to traditionally well-known characters from the region's as well as the Islamic history. Here are some examples:

Name		Nickname	
Mohammed – m7ammad	محمد	bu jasim	بو جاسم
Ibrahim	ابراهيم	bu khalil	بو خليل
Abdulrahman – 3abder-ra7man	عبد الرحمن	bu 3ouf	بو عوف
Ahmed – 'a7mad	أحمد	bu sh-hab	بو شهاب
Fatima – faTmah	فاطمة	'umm 3elii	أم علي
Ayesha – 3ayshah	عايشة	'umm 3abdallah	أم عبد الله
Maryam	مريم	'umm 3iisa	أم عيسى
Hamad-7amad	حمد	bu sh-hab	بو شهاب
Hamdan-7amdan	حمدان	bu rashid	بو راشد
Khalifa-kheliifah	خليفة	bu-7meid	بو حميد
Said- s3iid	سعيد	bu 3askuur	بو عسكور
Ali-3eli	علي	bu 7esan	بو حسن
Tariq -Tarig	طارق	bu ziyad	بو زياد
Khalid- khalid	خالد	bu waliid	بو وليد
Seif- seif	سيف	bu hannad	بو هناد

Khalfan-*khalfan*	خلفان	*bu 3jeil*	بو عجيل
Jumaa'- *yem3ah*	جمعة	*bu khammas*	بو خماس
Thani- *thani*	ثاني	*bu 7anni*	بو حنّي
Yaqub- *ya3guub*	يعقوب	*bu yousef*	بو يوسف
Abdel Aziz-*3abdel 3aziiz*	عبد العزيز	*bu s3uud*	بو سعود
Sultan-*selTan*	سلطان	*bu mayed*	بو مايد
Khalil- *khaliil*	خليل	*bu ibrahiim*	بو ابراهيم
Rahma- *ra7mah / r7amah*	رحمة	*bu jabir*	بو جابر
Salim- *salim*	سالم	*bu ghneim*	بو غنيم

Additionally, *'ubu* and *'umm* are used to refer to people using features / objects that distinguish them. Unlike nicknames linked to names of individuals, this applies to all ages and not only adults.

Feature / Object		Nickname
3yuun wsa3 Wide eyes	عيون وساع	*'umm 3yuun wsa3* (the one "female" with the wide eyes) = The male owner of wide eyes
sha3ar bin-nii Brown Hair	شعر بني	*'umm sha3ar bin-nii* (the one "female" with the brown eyes)
qamiiS 'a7mar Red shirt	قميص أحمر	*'ubu qamiiS 'a7mar* (the one "male" with the red shirt)
sa3ah zarga Blue watch	ساعة زرقا	*'ubu saa3ah zarqa* (the one "male" with the blue watch)
'il-3ebah 'is-soadah The black cloak	العباه السودا	*'umm 'il-3abah 'is-sodah* (the one "female" with the black cloak)
say-yarah 'umm 'arba3 biiban Car with four doors	سيارة أم أربع بيبان	*Say-yara 'umm 'arba3 biiban* (the car with with four doors)

Cognates — كلمات لها أصل أجنبي

Meaning المعنى	Transliteraton	Word الكلمة
Floating tube	*tyuub*	تيوب
I check	*'achay-yik*	أشيّك
Driver	*dreiwel*	دريول
Pick-up truck	*'il-bikab*	البيكاب
Oil	*'aayl*	آيل
Aerial, Antenna	*'aryal*	أريل
Sponge	*'isfanj = sfanj*	إسفنج = سفنج
Olympic	*'olimbi*	أولمبي
Sugar	*shekar*	شكر
Battery	*baT-Tariy-yah*	بطارية
Pasha	*basha*	باشه
Back player (in soccer)	*bak*	باك
Gasoline	*banziin*	بانزين
Petroleum	*betroal*	بترول
Power	*ba-war*	باور
Pajamas	*bijama*	بجامة
Tip	*bakhshiish*	بخشيش
Parliament	*barlaman*	برلمان
Biscuits, Cookies	*beskout*	بسكوت
Balcony	*balakoanah*	بلكونة
Billiards	*bilyard*	بليارد
Buffet	*buufei*	بوفيه
Beer	*biira*	بيرة
Insurance	*biima*	بيمة
Bus	*baS*	باص
Packet	*bakeit*	باكيت
Potatoes	*beTaT*	بطاط
Plastic	*blastiik*	بلاستيك
Pump	*bamb*	بمب

To go flat	banchar	بنشر
Powder	boudr	بودر
Pipe	beib	بيب
Tank (Water or gasoline)	tanki	تانكي
Car tire	tayir	تاير
Test, Examination	tra-y	تراي
Television	telfezyuun	تلفزيون
Telephone	telefuun	تليفون
Tanker car	tankar	تنكر
He tightened	tay-yat	تيت
Gypsum	jibs	جبس
Schedule	jadwal	جدول
Cigarette	segara	سيقارة
	jegara	
Matches, Match sticks	chabriit	كبريت
Chocolate	chakliit	تشكليت
Spoon	khashuuga	خاشوقة
Diploma	dibloam	دبلوم
Dozen	darzan	درزن
Doctor	daktoar	دكتور
		دختور دختر
Dynamite	diinamiit	ديناميت
Retouching	retuush	رتوش
Male secretary	sikerteir	سكرتير
Circus	sirk	سيرك
Cinema	senema	سينما
Shovle	sheiwal	شيول
Soap	Sabuun	صابون
Tomatoes	TemaT	طماط
Foul	fawil	فاول
Film	film	فلم
Physics	fiizya	فيزيا
Camera	keimara	كاميرا
Card	kart	كرت

Carbon	*karboan*	كربون
Coupon	*couboan*	كوبون
Cumin	*kam-muun*	كمون
Air conditioning	*kandeishin*	كنديشن
Cash	*kash*	كاش
Cake	*keik*	كيك
Kilogram, Kilometer	*keilo*	كيلو
Chemistry	*kiimya*	كيميا
Gas, Kerosene	*ghaz*	غاز
To cancel	*kansal*	كنسل
Exhaust	*kzuuz*	كزوز
Counselor	*qunSol*	قنصل
Liter	*letir*	لتر
London	*landan*	لندن
Driver Licence	*leisen*	ليسن
March	*maris*	مارس
Brand, Make	*markah*	ماركة
Machine	*makiina*	ماكينة
Meter	*meter*	متر
May	*mayo*	مايو
Music	*muusiiqa*	موسيقى
Mall	*moal*	مول
Yard (Measure)	*war*	وار
Jasmine	*yasmiin*	ياسمين

Cognates

In the chart above, you may have noticed the words that sound English. The creative nature of Arabic allows adoption of words from other languages. For instance, in spoken Arabic, many foreign words and are used by speakers. Such words include أشيّك *'achay-yik* "I check", أتيّت *'atay-yit* "I tighten", أديّم *'aday-yim* "I dim the light on and off", أسيّف *'asay-yiv* "I save", أبركن "I park".